STRAWBERRY

Production, Economics and Value Chain Analysis

The Authors

Dr. Shiv Prakash is currently Lecturer, Swami Keshwanand College Gramothan Vidhyapeeth, Sangaria, Affiliated College of Swami Keshwanand Rajasthan Agricultural University, Bikaner Rajasthan, India. He has a wide research/extension/ teaching experience and worked in different institute of repute *viz.*, Planning Office, Sirsa, Haryana, India, District Horticulture Office, Fatehabad, Haryana, India, District Horticulture Office, Sirsa, Haryana, India, Guru Kashi University, Talwandi Sabo, Punjab, India. He is teaching Agriculture Graduate Students. He is teach all graduate subjects *viz.*, Fundamental of Agricultural Economics, Production Economics, Farm Management and Resource Economics, Agricultural Marketing, Agricultural Finance and Cooperation and also teach Statistics. He has published 15 research papers and 5 popular articles national journals of repute, 01 book chapters, and 01 edited book. He has participated and presented papers and posters in many national and international seminars, workshops, symposium and conferences.

Dr. Debashis Sarkar is a Professor and Head at the Department of Agricultural Economics, Institute of Agriculture, Visva-Bharati, Sriniketan, West Bengal. He also served as Professor & Director, Agro-Economic Research Centre, Visva-Bharati for two years (2011-2013). He is an active researcher and has been teaching for the last 29 years. He has completed many research projects sponsored by UGC, ICAR-NIAP, Directorate of Jute Development, Government of India, Directorate of Crop Production, Government of India, and Directorate of PPQ&S, Government of India. He has published nine books (four edited) and numerous research papers in reputed national and international peer-reviewed professional journals.

STRAWBERRY

Production, Economics and Value Chain Analysis

– Authors –

Shiv Prakash

Lecturer and Head,
Department of Agricultural Economics
Swami Keshwanand College G.V., Sangaria (Raj)

Debashis Sarkar

Professor and Head
Department of Agricultural Economics
Palli Siksha Bhavana, Visva-Bharati, Sri Niketan, West Bengal

BIOTECH

2022

BIOTECH BOOKS®

ISBN 978-81-7622-504-5

Published by: **BIOTECH BOOKS®**
4762-63/23, Ansari Road, Darya Ganj,
New Delhi - 110 002
Phone: 09899295259, 011-43003222
E-mail: biotechbooks@yahoo.co.in
Website: www.biotechbooks.in

Typeset at: **Classic Computer Services**
Delhi - 110 035

Printed at: **Replika Press Pvt. Ltd.**

PRINTED IN INDIA

Preface

Indian Agriculture has traversed through peaks and troughs of technology success and failure, impact of institutional policies both in the national and international level, vagaries of nature in the form of flood, drought and climate change in course of history. Agriculture directly engages 70 per cent of the population and contributes nearly 14 per cent to the Indian economy, which has come down from nearly 50 per cent at the time of independence. At a time when the population feared starvation, the Green Revolution saved the Indian agriculture through its HYVs and intensive input use policies in the 60s. The food grains production escalated tremendously during the next two decades and then the growth recorded a slump period. The problems faced were mono-cropping which resulted in inputs unresponsiveness, soil degradation and loss of biodiversity; rapid destruction of natural resources, migration of youths in search of employments, lack of market, glut in production and lack of proper storage to carry-over the surplus and a multitude of other problems. Therefore, it is need of hour that farmers have to shift from mono cropping patterns to diversification like cultivation of high values crops *viz.*, protected cultivation of vegetables and fruits which leads towards doubling of farmers' income. Unrelenting research from research institutes and universities and Government policies have succeeded in mitigating some of these effects in the past. With the development of ICTs, agricultural marketing has been taken a level ahead with e-NAM, an initiative taken by government to unify the agricultural markets at national level. As a result of the Government incentive on pulse and fruit crops area increase 10 per cent from last two decades. This proves that albeit the agricultural sector is replete with multitude of problems, relentless effort has been provided from researchers and policy makers from all over the country to solve the national problems. This book has been compiled from the work done by research scholar at the Department of Agricultural Economics, Palli Siksha Bhavana (Institute of Agriculture), Visva-Bharati, Sriniketan, Birbhum, West Bengal.

Dr. Shiv Prakash

Dr. Debashis Sarkar

Contents

List of Figures

List of Tables

Chapter 1

Introduction

1.1 Introduction

Horticulture is an important industry among the land based agricultural systems. It comprises the cultivation of large varieties of fruits such as mango, apple, citrus, papaya, pineapple, guava, strawberry, jackfruits, pomegranate, ber *etc.* Among the horticultural crops, fruit plays a very important role in terms of economic development, employment generation, nutritional security and the overall economic growth of various countries including India. The major fruit producing countries in the world are China (21.21 per cent), India (12.60 per cent), Brazil (5.90 per cent), USA (4.10 per cent), Indonesia (2.70 per cent), Philippines (2.50 per cent), Mexico (2.50 per cent), Turkey (2.30 per cent), Spain (2.20 per cent), Italy (2.10 per cent) and others (4.80 per cent). India has been predominantly an agrarian economy since time immemorial. Agriculture occupies the central place in rural life and it continues to be mainstay of our economy even today as 70 per cent of populations depend on agriculture as a mean of livelihood. It was evident that its contribution towards the national income declined from 28.97 per cent during 1990-91 to 16.00 per cent during 2011-12 (Kumar, 2013). In spite of this it is still considered as the backbone of Indian economy. It has a diverse climate suitable for cultivation of large varieties of fruits. It ranks second in production of fruits in the world, after China.

India's diverse climate ensures availability of all varieties of fresh fruits and vegetables. It ranks second in fruits and vegetables production in the world, after China. India produced 90.18 million MT of fruits in area of fruits 6.30 million ha during 2015-16 (GoI, 2016). Hence, India developed a lot in horticulture sector, consequently. Its horticulture production has increased by 90.26 per cent in the last thirteen years. Of the total fruit area in India, mango, banana, papaya and citrus share the major (more than 60 per cent) part with the production of more than 70 per cent of the total fruit production of the country. The horticulture sector has been a driving force in stimulating a healthy growth trend in Indian agriculture.

India is currently producing 286.19 MT of horticulture produce from an area of 24.47 million ha. Over the last fifteen years, the area under horticulture grew by about 47.48 per cent which boost production by 96.31 per cent, higher growth rate in horticulture was brought about by improvement in productivity of horticulture crops, which increased by about 33.11 per cent between 2001-02(16.59 Million Ha area and 145.78 MT production) 2015-16 (24.47 Million ha area and 286.19 MT production) (GoI, 2016).

The major destinations for exports of Indian fruits are UAE, Bangladesh, Malaysia, UK, Netherland, Pakistan, Saudi Arabia, Sri Lanka and Nepal. Though India's share in the global market is still less than 1 per cent only, there is increasing demand of horticultural produce from the country. This has occurred due to concurrent developments in the areas of state-of-the-art cold chain infrastructure and quality assurance measures. Fruits are man's oldest food and its cultivation is as old as human civilization itself. It is mostly consumed as fresh, processed product and use for making various medicinal purposes. It is the prime source of vitamins and minerals which are essential for human body to resist the diseases, its role in improving the environment and aesthetic value is an added advantage. Adequate eating of fruits likely to reduce the chronic diseases and provides sound health and happiness to human being. As per the Indian Council of Medical Research (ICMR, 2010) the per capita requirement of fruits is at least 92 grams is recommended per head per day. However on the contrary, the per-capita consumption of fruits in India is only 46 grams per day (Sachdeva*et al.*, 2013). Eating a diet rich in vegetables and fruits as part of an overall healthy diet may reduce risk for heart disease, including heart attack, stroke, protect against certain types of cancers. Vegetables and fruits containing fiber may reduce the risk of heart disease, obesity and type II diabetes. Vegetables and fruits rich in potassium as part of an overall healthy diet may lower blood pressure, and may also reduce the risk of developing kidney stones and help to decrease bone loss, and lower in calories per cup instead of some other higher-calorie food may be useful in helping to lower calorie intake (http://www.choosemyplate.gov).

Strawberry is known to be originated from France and belongs to Rosacea, Rose family (*Fragaria X ananassa*). The major known cultivar varieties of strawberry are *ofra, camarosa, chandler, sweet charlie, fair fox, black more, elista*and *seascape*. It is a fair source of vitamin C, 100 g edible portion of strawberry contains 89 g water, 0.07 g protein, 0.5 g fats, 8.4 g carbohydrates and 59 mg ascorbic acid and commercially consumed as fresh fruits, processed products like ice cream, soft drink, confectionary and chewing gum and preserved like james, jellies, and squashes which can be used in off-season (Galletta and Bringhurst, 1995). It is one among the fruits having an immense potential and having high economic value. Its cultivation is widely practiced around the world, at present the world's leading producers of strawberry are USA 30.4 per cent, Turkey 7.0 per cent, Spain 6.0 per cent, Egypt 5.5 per cent and Mexico 5.3 per cent (FAOSTAT, 2015). In India, strawberry cultivation is confined to hilly region of the country. In view of good returns from Strawberry, its cultivation is becoming increasingly popular in west and north India, especially in Maharashtra, Himachal Pradesh, Haryana and Punjab. It is suitable for semiarid and subtropical zone, ideal fruit crop for Maharashtra, Himachal Pradesh, Haryana and Punjab. India is the second largest producer of fruit in the world after China. Its share in the world's output of fruits is 11 per cent because of its varied agro-climatic conditions. Recently, strawberry is successfully being cultivated in plain area of Maharashtra, around Pune, Nashik, Sangali towns and Hisar and Bhiwani districts of Haryana state.

The state of Haryana has ample scope of production of fruits, vegetables, and flowers, spices mushroom, medicinal and aromatic plants. The cultivation of horticulture crops is highly specialized, technical and remunerative venture as compared to traditional crops being grown by the farmers. Apart from this, majority of Horticulture crops, being perishable in nature, requires systematic planning for their development. Horticulture development has assumed greater importance in recent years since this sector has been identified as remunerative for diversification of land use which provides increased employment opportunities, better return per unit area besides filling the nutritional gaps. Farmers in Haryana have also started taking up horticulture crops as a separate viable economic activity, with a view to give a boost to the growth of horticulture in the state. Haryana is one of the 29 states in India, situated in North India. It was carved out of the former state of East Punjab on 1 November 1966 on a linguistic basis. It stands 21st in terms of its area, which is spread about 44,212 km^2. It has tremendously developed itself in terms of economy and progressing in production of fruits and vegetables. It is known as an agrarian state, as most of the people depend on agriculture. The state having rich source of horticulture crops such as fruits, vegetables *etc.* The agro climatic condition of Haryana is suitable for growing of many kinds of fruits *viz.*, Grapes, Kinnow, Malta, Mango, Ber, Guava, Peach, and Papaya. Suitable varieties are popular among farmers. There is a great scope of increase the area under Horticulture crops.

The area under fruit crops during 2015-16 in the state has been recorded as 60.92 ha with a production of 737.82 MT (GoH, 2016). Among the fruits, strawberry is one of the most important fruit grown in the state which gives an immense income to the livelihood of the farmer. It is known as a low volume high value crop and grows well under protected and open condition. It can be easily grown in state of Haryana. It gives quickest return in short time than any other fruit crops. The total area under strawberry in the state during 2015-16 was 140 ha with a total production of 1651 MT (GoH, 2016). Strawberry from the state is being sold in Delhi market. It is also exported to Bhutan, Nepal, Bangladesh and various other countries.

1.2 Statement of the Problem

Indian agriculture is diversifying into the production of high value fruits, also providing an increasing role to small holding farmers as most of the cultivable land in the country belongs to small category of farmer. Thus, in a holistic way, horticulture can be promoted as a means of agro-diversification for the second Green Revolution, providing the much needed impetus to the growth of agricultural sector, through increase in trade, income and employment. With the launch of National Horticulture Mission (NHM) in 2005 the production of horticulture crop was found to be increased with the increase in area. The total domestic demand for fruits is expected to increase of 25.47 million ton by 2020. This huge demand of fruits for domestic consumption is a challenge to meet out by the country. A long with this, the goal to produce horticultural products for exports, can act as an engine of growth to the agricultural sector. However, growth in the fruit production and processing sub-sectors provides employment opportunities and income generation.

Haryana, one of the 29 states of country which has an immense scope for strawberry production as the climatic condition is highly favourable for the crop. The growers also can receive comparatively higher profit on selling the fruit due to its high value in nature. Hence, producing strawberry is becoming an alternative source of income for the farmers of the state. But unfortunately, despite of strawberry being profitable, it could spread and it might be due to unaware about the profitability of the crop. They are also not well aware about the proper marketing channel and marketing strategy to be followed for getting the due share of producers in consumer's rupee. Shortage of runners (seedling) which are not readily available in their farm has become a matter of concern in the recent past. On the contrary, organised market for strawberry made the traders/middlemen the major players in marketing of strawberry. Keeping all these into consideration, the present study on strawberry cultivation is an imperative as there is no such type of study carried out in this regard.

Hence, keeping in view the importance of the crop and the various problematic situations associated with strawberry cultivation, the present research study entitled "Economics of Production and Marketing of Strawberry in Haryana, India" has been undertaken with the following specific objectives.

1.3 Objectives

The specific objectives of the study are:

1. To work out the economics of strawberry in Haryana state;
2. To study the marketing practices and channels involved in marketing of strawberry in the state;
3. To estimate the marketing costs, margins and price spread for the strawberry; and
4. To identify the problems faced by the producers and traders in the production and marketing of strawberry.

1.4 Rationale of the Study

Strawberry is one of the most important temperate and sub-tropical fruit crop in India. The most important strawberry growing states in India are Maharashtra, Haryana, Meghalaya, Himachal Pradesh, Uttaranchal, Mizoram, Punjab, Delhi and Rajasthan. Subtropical area in Jammu has also the potential to growth the crop under irrigated condition. It is an important fruit owing to its high nutritive, medicinal and having higher productivity per unit area in the wasteland, particularly in un-irrigated sandy soil which are available in plenty in the country. In view of good returns from strawberry, its cultivation is becoming increasingly popular in west and north India especially in Maharashtra, Himachal Pradesh, Haryana and Punjab.

Haryana is the 2nd largest producers of strawberry after Maharashtra. Commercial cultivation of strawberry is becoming important in Haryana. Hence, the state has potential to increase the area and production under strawberry for betterment of livelihood of the farmers by realizing its profitability.

The production process is not considered as complete until the product does not reach to end users. Marketing of agricultural produce has to play a significant role in Indian economy. The study of marketing is very important in which producers' share in consumers' rupee, various channels involved in the process of marketing of strawberry, extent of margins earned by the intermediaries, cost incurred by various marketing functions during the marketing process, the study of marketing efficiency of channels as well as various markets of strawberry are involved. Further, the field level constraints/problems faced by producers and traders of strawberry can provide way forward to take appropriate policies for betterment of cultivation of any crop.

1.5 Limitations of the Study

Very rare studies in the field of social sciences dealing with human behaviour are free from some limitations and sometime they are beyond the control of researcher. The present study has limitations of the time and other resources available with the student researcher. The findings of the study are restricted based on a sample of 200 strawberry growers and one market. Hence, the sweeping generalisation on the basis of results outcome of the study should be done with some reservations. The finding of the study can be universally generalised with identical socio-economic and agro-ecological conditions. Further, the expressed opinion of the respondent, in the study may not be free from personal bias and prejudices. However, considerable care and thought have been exercised in making the study as accurate and systematic as possible.

1.6 Organisation of the study

The thesis has been organized into seven chapters. The first chapter represents the background, problem of statement, rational of the study and limitation of the study. The second discusses on review of literature based on previous related research findings. The third chapter represents research methodology adopted to carry out the present investigation. The fourth chapter discusses the socio-economic profile of the study area and the respondents. Results and discussion are discussed in chapter five. Chapter six outlined with summary and conclusion of the entire investigation. Finally, the future scope of research has been discussed in chapter seven.

Chapter 2

Research Methodology

This chapter is concerned with the description on research methods and techniques followed for carrying out the study. It also describes design of research, sampling design, methods of data collection, the empirical measures developed and techniques used to measure the variables and concept and finally the statistical procedures employed in the analysis of data.

2.1 Design of Research

The study has been conducted based upon the survey method. In this method, the investigator sampled a group of individuals, and their responses to the questions were asked and recorded. This was done through personal interviewing method. The investigator used pre-structured scheduled to collect the relevant information from the individuals. More specifically in this method, the interviewer contacted the respondents, asked questions and filled-in the survey schedules according to the responses of the respondents.

Table 2.1: Area and Production of Strawberry in Haryana

Sl. No.	*Districts*	*Area (in Hectares)*		*Production (in Tonnes)*	
		2014-15	*2015-16*	*2014-15*	*2015-16*
1.	Hisar	91 (64.54)	85 (62.50)	860 (62.18)	900 (65.03)
2.	Bhiwani	35 (24.82)	36 (26.47)	320 (23.14)	390 (28.18)
3.	Sirsa	4 (2.84)	1 (0.74)	48 (3.47)	18 (1.30)
4.	Fatehabad	4 (2.84)	0 (0.00)	68 (4.92)	0 (0.00)
5.	Karnal	2 (1.42)	1 (0.74)	30 (2.17)	13 (0.94)
6.	Narnaul	2 (1.42)	0 (0.00)	17 (1.23)	0 (0.00)
7.	Ambala	0 (0.00)	2 (1.47)	0 (0.00)	23 (1.67)
8.	Sonipat	0 (0.00)	1 (0.74)	0 (0.00)	20 (1.44)

Sl. No.	Districts	Area (in Hectares)		Production (in Tonnes)	
		2014-15	2015-16	2014-15	2015-16
9.	Gurgram	0 (0.00)	10 (7.35)	0 (0.00)	20 (1.44)
10.	Rest of All Districts	3 (2.12)	0 (0.00)	40 (2.89)	0 (0.00)
	Total	**141 (100.00)**	**136 (100.00)**	**1383 (100.00)**	**1384 (100.00)**

Note: Figures in brackets are the percentage over total.

Source: Directorate of Horticulture, Government of Haryana, Panchkula, 2016.

Table 2.2: Selected Villages by Selected Blocks and Districts, Haryana

District	Name of Block	Selected Villages
Hisar	Hisar-1	Sahadawa
		Satrod Khurd
Bhiwani	Siwani	Chanana
		Siwani

2.2 Selection of Districts

The basic considerations for the selection of the districts are discussed in this section. Haryana is divided into four divisions for administrative purposes; they are Ambala, Gurgram, Hisar and Rohtak. Within these divisions there are 22 districts, 47 sub-divisions, 67 tehsils, 45 sub-tehsils and 116 blocks. There are total 81 cities and towns in Haryana and 6,759 villages. As per the latest available secondary information, the area and production of strawberry are highest in Hisar and Bhiwani districts in Haryana (Table 2.1). Thus, Hisar and Bhiwani districts of Haryana were selected purposively for the present study.

2.3 Selection of Blocks

Hisar district comprises of nine blocks. Out of these nine blocks, Hisar-1 block was selected purposively based on the highest area and production of strawberry. Bhiwani district comprises of seven blocks. Similarly out of these seven blocks, Siwani block was selected purposively based on the highest area and production of strawberry.

2.4 Selection of Villages

A list of all villages of selected blocks of both the selected district was prepared with the area under strawberry of individual farmer. Finally, two villages namely Sahadawa, Satrod Khurd from Hisar-1 block of Hisar district and Chanana and Siwani villages from Siwani block of Bhiwani district were selected randomly for the present study (Table 2.2).

2.5 Selection of Respondents

A comprehensive list of total strawberry grower of the four selected villages has been prepared along and then categorised into three categories based on their land holdings *viz.*, small (up to 2.0 ha), medium (2.10 to 4.00) and large (>4.00 ha). It has been found that there are 316 strawberry growers in these four villages (Table 2.3). Finally, 200 strawberry growers was selected by employing the probability proportional to size (Table 2.4 and Figure 2.1) as the ultimate sample unit of the study. The village-wise distribution of strawberry growers according to different categories is presented in Table 2.5.

Table 2.3: Total Number of Strawberry Growers by Size of Holding

Categories	*Size of Land Holding (Ha.)*	*Number of Growers*
Small	Up to 2 ha.	167
Medium	2.10-4ha.	87
Large	>4ha	62
Total		**316**

Table 2.4: Classification of Strawberry Grower

Categories	*Size of Land Holding (Ha.)*	*No. Selected Growers*
Small	Up to 2 ha.	105
Medium	2.10-4ha.	55
Large	>4ha	40
Total		**200**

Table 2.5: Distribution of Selected Strawberry Growers by Selected Villages

Name of Village	*Category of Strawberry Growers*			*Total*
	Small	*Medium*	*Large*	
Sahadwa	50	07	15	72
Satrod Khurd	23	15	12	50
Chanana	18	22	10	50
Siwani	14	11	03	28
Total	**105**	**55**	**40**	**200**

2.6 Selection of Market

It has been found that Azadpur market is the major market for strawberry both for Hisar and Bhiwani districts because more than 80 per cent of the produce of these districts is merchandised through this market. Thus Azadpur market was selected purposively to study the different market functionaries associated with marketing of strawberry. While collecting the primary information, it has been found that four major channels are connected towards marketing of strawberry in Azadpur market which is furnished below.

(i) Channel I: Producer → Commission Agent → Retailer → Consumer

(ii) Channel II: Producer → Wholesaler → Retailer → Consumer

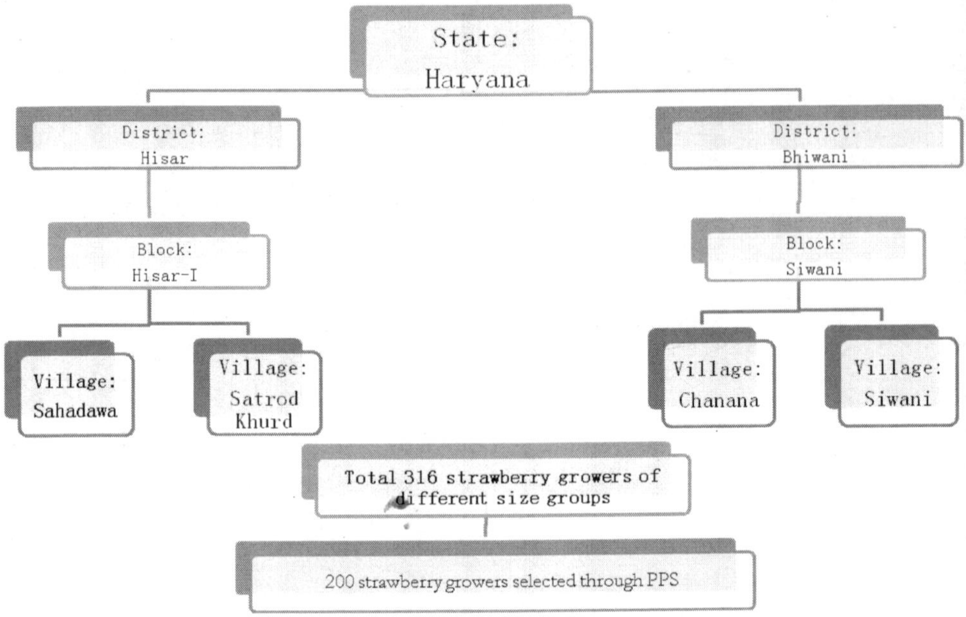

Figure 2.1: Sampling Plan for Selection of Respondent.

(iii) Channel III: Producer → Retailer → Consumer

(iv) Channel IV: Producer → Consumer

The major identified channels are studied in depth in order to conducting a comprehensive study on marketing and marketing functionaries of strawberry in the study area.

2.7 Tools and Techniques of Data Collection

2.7.1 Developing and Pre-testing of Survey Schedule

The primary data has been collected with the help of survey schedule specially constructed for the purpose of this study, keeping in view the focus, objectives and variables. The entire draft schedule has been pre-tested with 10 per cent non-sample respondents before administering into the actual respondents. Pre-testing has been done to ensure the validity of the survey schedule under local condition. Accordingly, after the completion of the pre-testing the survey schedule has been revised and improved with appropriate wordings and contents.

2.7.2 Interviewing and Data Collection

Primary data includes both quantitative as well as qualitative information based on long term experiences of the strawberry growers. Economic analysis essentially requires both quantitative and qualitative information of the households over a time horizon. Both have their advantages and disadvantages. Quantitative information provide large amount of information which are amenable to statistical analysis but the focus is always on current circumstances. While qualitative information are difficult to analyse when the sample size is too large. Therefore striking a balance between quantitative questions and open ending qualitative questions is important. Information on linked entities is also important. Therefore, attempt has been made in using inputs from household survey, village survey and secondary information at higher scales. To collect the information from different types of strawberry growers prevailing in the study area, primary survey was carried out during 2015-16. This study also used secondary information on several aspects from various published sources. Secondary data on major indicators at various levels are collected from different published reports of the government, other published works like research articles, journals, newspapers *etc.*

The primary data pertains to the general information, assets, cropping pattern, details on various inputs used in strawberry cultivation *viz.*, runner (seedling), fertilizers, manure, plant protection, labour and cultivation practices such as; land preparation, source of irrigation, drip irrigation, inter-cultural operations, harvesting and labour used in strawberry cultivation and problems faced by the producer during the crop year 2015-16. Data on disposal of strawberry, marketing cost incurred by various intermediaries in marketing of strawberry, purchase and selling price of the producers, purchase price of the consumers were also collected. A close-ended questionnaire was also used to record the problems faced by the different intermediaries during the marketing process of strawberry.

2.7.3 The Survey Schedule and Village Survey

2.7.3.1 The Survey Schedule

Household is an economic unit in socio-economic model. To obtain basic information from the sampled households, comprehensive schedule has been used that covers:

- ☆ Demographic features, educational aspects and occupation
- ☆ Detailed information regarding size of land holding
- ☆ Detailed information regarding status of irrigation
- ☆ Detailed information regarding cropping pattern
- ☆ Detailed information regarding cultivation practices of strawberry
- ☆ Detailed information regarding cost of cultivation of strawberry
- ☆ Detailed information regarding market functionaries involved in the marketing process of strawberry
- ☆ Detailed information regarding marketing functions and cost involved in the marketing process of strawberry
- ☆ Opinions/suggestions regarding problems faced by the producers and traders in the production and marketing of strawberry.

2.7.3.2 Village Survey

Village level information has been collected from group interactions, taking inputs from Panchayat and government officials. Discussions have been made with village heads, important decision makers, and government persons living in the selected villages or having knowledge about the villages. They were thoroughly interviewed to collect information about the village, its resources, problems, *etc.*

2.8 Analytical Techniques

The overview of the procedures applied in this study is presented below. After scrutiny, the collected data has been processed to fulfil the various objectives laid down for the study. The processing of data has been done by manual tabulation as well as by the help of computer. However, there are several restrictions that may limit the usefulness of applying a management technique to a decision-making problem. They include the validity of a given technique to a problem situation, the resources that are required for its use and the effectiveness with which the information derived from it is communicated to the decision-makers in farming, extension, research and administration. The evolution and practical application of management techniques to decision-making in developed countries have been such that while the sophistication and the computational capabilities of analysts have consistently grown, there has developed alienation between the developers of these techniques and their clients. This has prevented widespread adoption of some potentially useful techniques to decision-making in agriculture.

In recent years, farmers are becoming more and more conscious about the costs and returns from agriculture in general and enterprises on one farm in particular. Farmer relates the price, which he receives for the produce in the market with his cost of production. In view of the rapid spread of technology in agriculture, farmers are required to face a severe competition, particularly when the farm produce is to be exported. One of the ways to survive in the competition as also to gain better profit is to have a lower cost of production. For this farm costing or working out the cost of production of crops/enterprises, is necessary. The farm costing is also useful to the farmers to keep watch on the expenditure which is increasing in the modern farming. In view of these, different cost concepts used in farm management studies have been employed for fruitful interpretation of the data. Similarly, the different types of marketing functions involved and marketing cost thereby has been calculated by employing the standard tools and techniques. The significance of the results obtained from the various techniques has been examined for generalization of the objectives.

2.9 Econometric and Statistical Tools Used

The following economic and statistical tools have been employed for precise and better analysis and interpretation of the data. These are briefly discussed as follows.

2.9.1 Costs and Returns from Strawberry Cultivation

To attain the first objective budgeting techniques and various cost concepts were applied. Among the cost, establishment cost and maintenance cost which includes cost A_1, cost A_2, cost B_1, cost B_2, cost C_1 and cost C_2 has been worked out.

2.9.1.1 Establishment Cost of Strawberry Orchard

Construction of plan in any business activity entails some initial cost. Such initial costs are called establishment cost in the business analysis. The establishment cost per hectare of strawberry cultivation has been estimated considering the quantity of inputs and labour used and their respective market price and wages prevailed in the study area. It includes the cost on pump set, drip irrigation, investment for on fencing *etc.*

2.9.1.2 Operational Cost

The operational costs include cost A_1, cost A_2, cost B_1, cost B_2, cost C_1 and cost C_2 which are known as cost concept. These various cost concepts were applied by Special Expert Committee Government of India (1980) which are summarized below:

Cost A

a) Value of hired human labour
b) Value of hired bullock labour
c) Value of owned bullock labour
d) Value of owned machinery labour
e) Value of hired machinery charges
f) Value of seed (both farm produced and purchased)
g) Value of insecticides and pesticides
h) Value of manure (owned and purchased)
i) Value of fertilizer
j) Depreciation on implements and farm buildings
k) Irrigation charges
l) Land revenue
m) Interest on working capital
n) Miscellaneous expenses (Artisans *etc.*)

Cost A_2: Cost A_1 + Rent paid for leased-in land

Cost B_1: Cost A_1 + Interest on value of owned fixed capital assets (excluding land)

Cost B_2: Cost B_1 + Rental value of owned land less land revenue + Rent paid for leased-in land

Cost C_1: Cost B_1 + Imputed value of family labour

Cost C_2: Cost B_2 + Imputed value of family labour

2.9.1.3 Various Concepts of Returns on Investment

(i) Gross Farm income (GFI) = Production   Price

(ii) Net return including family labour = GFI – Total cost including family labour

(iii) Net return excluding family labour = GFI – Total cost excluding family labour

(iv) Farm business income = GFI – Cost A_2

(v) Family labour income = GFI – Cost B_2

(vi) Net farm income = GFI – Cost C_2

(vii) Farm investment income = Farm business income – wages of family labour

2.9.1.4 Benefit Cost Ratio (BCR)

(i) On the basis of the total cost: Gross Farm income (GFI) Cost C_2

(ii) On the basis of paid out cost: Gross Farm income (GFI) Cost A_1

2.9.2 Marketing of Strawberry

To study the existing marketing pattern of strawberry in the study area, disposal pattern of strawberry grower to major market through various marketing agencies was studied. The marketing cost, margins and efficiency as well as the price spread of different channels in markets has been worked out.

2.9.2.1 Marketing Cost

Marketing cost is the cost incurred in moving the produce from the point of production to the point of consumption, *i.e.*, the cost of performing the various marketing functions and of operating various agencies. The following formula was used:

$$C = C_f + C_{m1} + C_{m2} + C_{m3} + \ldots + C_{mn}$$

where,

C = Total cost of marketing of the commodity

C_f = Cost paid by the producer

C_{mi} = Cost incurred by the ith middleman

i = 1 to n

2.9.2.2 Marketing Margin of Middlemen

It isthe difference between the total payments (costs + purchase price) and receipts (sale price) of the middlemen (the agency) for an equivalent quantity of farm produce. This was calculated by using the following formula:

$$A_{mi} = P_{Ri} - (P_{Pi} + C_{mi})$$

where,

A_{mi} = Absolute marketing margin of ith middlemen

P_{Ri} = Total value receipts per unit

P_{Pi} = Purchase value per unit

C_{mi} = Cost incurred on marketing per unit

2.9.2.3 Percentage Margin of Middleman

The percentage margin of middleman was worked out by using the following formula:

$$(P_{mi}) = \frac{P_{Ri} - (P_{pi} + C_{mi})}{P_{Ri}} \times 100$$

where,

P_{Ri} = Total value of receipts per unit of produce (sale price)
P_{pi} = Purchase value of goods per unit of produce (purchase price)
C_{mi} = Cost incurred in marketing per unit

The margin thus calculated includes the profit of the middleman and the returns

2.9.2.4 Price Spread

It is the difference between the price paid by consumer and the price received by the producer for an equivalent quantity of farm produce (Acharya, 2001). In the present study price spread was calculated by using the following formula:

$$P_s = \frac{P_f}{P_r} \times 100$$

where,

P_s = Producer's share in the consumer rupee.
P_f = Price received by the farmer per unit of output.
P_r = Retail price per unit of output (₹ /kg)

and,

$$P_f = P_A - C_F$$

Where,

P_f = Net price received by strawberry producer (₹ /q)
P_A = Wt. avg. price received by strawberry producer (₹ /q)
C_F = Marketing cost incurred by strawberry producer (₹ /q)

2.9.2.5 Producer's Price

It is the price received by strawberry producer at the time of first sale. This is equal to the wholesale price at the primary assembly centre, minus the charges borne by the producer in selling the strawberry. The producer's price was calculated by using the following formula (Acharya and Agarwal, 2011).

$$P_F = P_A - C_F$$

where,

P_F = Producer's price

P_A = Wholesale price in the primary assembling market

C_F = Marketing cost incurred by the producer

2.9.2.6 Producer's Share in Consumer's Rupee

It is the price received by the strawberry producer at which it is expressed as the percentage of the retail price *i.e.,* the price paid by consumer. However, to attain the producer's share in consumer's rupee (P_S) the following formula was used (Acharya and Agarwal, 2011).

$$P_S = \frac{P_F}{P_r} \times 100$$

where,

P_S = Producers' share in consumers' rupee

P_F = Price of the producer

P_r = Retail price

2.9.2.7 Marketing Efficiency

Marketing efficiency is the ratio of market output to market input. An increase in this ratio represents improved efficiency and a decrease denotes reduced efficiency. In the present study, marketing efficiency was calculated by using Acharya's Modified Marketing Efficiency method *i.e.*

$$E = \frac{O}{I} \times 100$$

where,

E = Index of marketing efficiency

O = Value added by the marketing system

I = Cost + margin' of marketing intermediaries

Acharya's modified marketing efficiency (MME)

$$MME = \frac{FP}{(MC + MM)}$$

where,

MME = Modified measure of Marketing Efficiency

FP = Price received by Farmers

MC = Marketing Cost

MM = Marketing Margin

2.9.3 Problems Faced by Producers and Traders of Strawberry

The information on various problems faced by producers and traders of strawberry in the study area were recorded from the respondents. Tabular analysis has been employed to examine the problems in cultivation and marketing of strawberry at the grass root levels.

Hanry Garrett's ranking technique was also used to evaluate the problems faced by the respondents. The orders of merit given by the respondents were converted in to rank by using the formula. To find out the most significant factor which influences the respondent, Garrett's ranking technique was used. As per this method, respondents have been asked to assign the rank for all factors and the outcomes of such ranking have been converted into score value with the help of following formula:

$$\text{Per cent composition} = \frac{100(\text{Rji} - 0.5)}{\text{Nji}}$$

where,

Rij = Rank given for the ith variable by j^{th} respondents

Nj = Number of variable ranked by j^{th} respondents

With the help of Garrett's table, the percent position has been estimated and converted into scores. Then for each factor, the scores of each individual are added and then total value of scores and mean value of score is calculated. The factors having highest mean value is considered to be the most important factor.

Chapter 3

Socio-economic Profile of the Study Area and the Respondents

3.1 State: Haryana

The small state of Haryana was founded in 1966 when the former state of Punjab was divided into Haryana and the modern Punjab. It is both the oldest and most modern of places. Delhi, Punjab, Rajasthan, Himachal Pradesh and Uttar Pradesh surround the state. The state was a major contributor to the "HaritKranti", the green revolution and is a good blend of traditional and modern cultures. Haryana is located in the north-west part of the country. Haryana is bound by Uttar Pradesh in the east, Punjab in the west, Himachal Pradesh in the north and Rajasthan in the South. The national capital territory of Delhi is next to Haryana. Haryana is situated between the latitude 30.30° North and longitude 74.60° East. Most of Haryana is in the plains with the Aravali mountain range starting its westward journey from here. The Yamuna is the only major river that passes through this small state, which is one of the greenest in the country. There is a very good network of canals throughout the state, giving it the much-needed impetus for agriculture, the mainstay of Haryana's economy. Its climate is arid to semi-arid with average rainfall of 354.5 mm. around -29 per cent rainfall is received during the month from July to September and the remaining rainfall is received during December to February. There are two agro climatic zones in the state. The north western part is suitable for Rice, Wheat, Vegetable and temperate fruits and the south western part is suitable for high quality agricultural produce, tropical fruits, exotic vegetables and herbal and medicinal plants. The total geographical area of the state is 4.42 m ha, which is 1.4 per cent of the geographical area of the country. The cultivable area is 3.7 m ha, which is 84 per cent of the geographical area of the state out of which 3.64 m ha *i.e.* 98 per cent is under cultivation. The gross cropped area of the state is 6.51m ha and net cropped area is 3.64 m ha with a cropping intensity of 184.91 per

Figure 3.1: Map of Haryana State, India.

cent (http://agriharyana.nic.in/ accessed on 04.02.2017). Haryana has 22 districts namely; Ambala, Bhiwani, Faridabad, Fatehabad, Gurgram, Hisar, Jhajjar, Jind, Kaithal, Karnal, Kurukshetra, Mahendergarh, Panchkula, Panipat, Rewari, Rohtak, Sirsa, Sonepat, Yamuna Nagar, Mewat, Palwal and CharkhiDadri. Among the districts Hisar and Bhiwani were selected as the area and production of strawberry has been reported highest.

Table 3.1: Geographical Area and Population of Hisar, Bhiwani and Haryana

District/ State	*Area in sq.kms.*	*Population*			*Density of Population/ sq.km*
		Rural	*Urban*	*Total*	
Hisar	3983.00 (9.01)	1190443 (68.26)	55348 (31.74)	1743931 (100.00)	438
Bhiwani	5140.00 (11.63)	1438388 (88.00)	196057 (12.00)	1634445 (100.00)	341
Haryana	44212.00 (100.00)	16509359 (65.12)	8,842103 (34.88)	25351462 (100.00)	**573**

Figures in parentheses represent the percentage over total population.

Source: Census of India, 2011.

Table 3.2: Land Use Oattern in Hisar, Bhiwani and Punjab-Haryana Plains (Per cent to total reporting area)

District/ Region	*Forest Land*	*Land not Available for Cultivation*	*Cultivable Wasteland*	*Current Fallow Land*	*Net Sown Area*
Hisar	0.00	9.88	0.00	12.10	78.02
Bhiwani	0.64	9.44	0.00	5.15	84.76
Region	3.51	10.95	0.90	2.80	**81.84**

Source: Statistical Abstract, Government of Haryana.

3.2 District: Hisar

Hisar district is one of the important and fast growing district of Haryana. Very hot summers and very cold winters can be experienced in the district. The maximum day temperature during the summer varies from 40 to 46 degree Celsius. During winter its ranges from 1.5 degree to 4 degree Celsius. The winds are strong and frequent during May to July. Normally the South Westerly current of summer monsoon brings the rains during July to September period. Intermittent dust storms are also common. According to the 2011 census the district had a population of 1,742,815 roughly equal to the nation of The Gambia or the US State of Nebraska. This gave it a ranking of 276th in India out of a total of 640 districts. The district has a population density of 438 inhabitants per square kilometre (1,130/sq mi). Its population growth rate over the decade 2001-2011 was 13.38 per cent. Hisar has a sex ratio of 871 females for every 1000 males, and a literacy rate of 73.2 per cent.

Haryanvi is the most spoken dialect in the district. Hisar is 98 per cent Hindu, only about 40,000 are Muslims, rest are mostly Jain and Sikhs. Hisar district is emerging district in production of strawberry where the area under strawberry was 85 ha with a production of 900 ton.

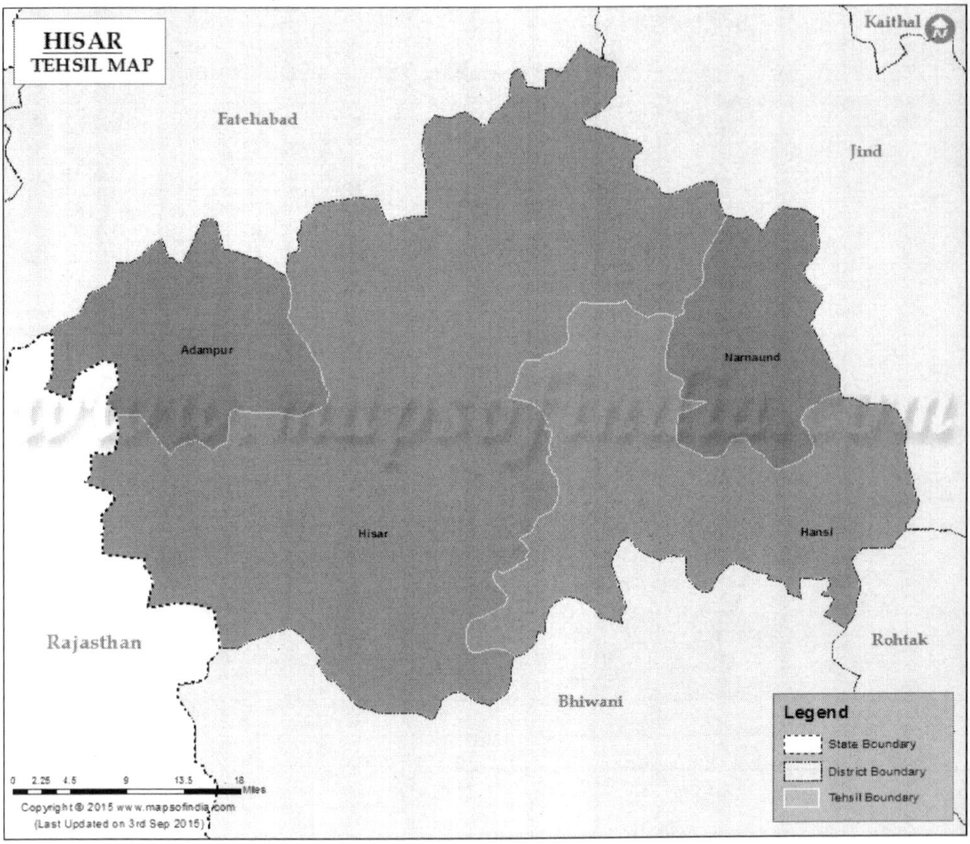

Figure 3.2: Map of Hisar District.

3.3 District: Bhiwani

District Bhiwani is situated between 28.19° and 29.05° North latitude and 75.26° and 76.28° East longitude. The Bhiwani district is surrounded by Hisar District on its North, some area of Jhunjunu and Churu District of Rajasthan on its west, Charkhi Dadri and Jhunjunu district on its south and District Rohtak on east. It is 124 Kilometre from Delhi and 285 Kilometre from Chandigarh. In North Region of the district there are Alluvial Plains and in South there were Semi -Desert with remnants of Aravali Range Mountains. The Soil is loom in the North region and sandy in the Southwest region of Bhiwani district.

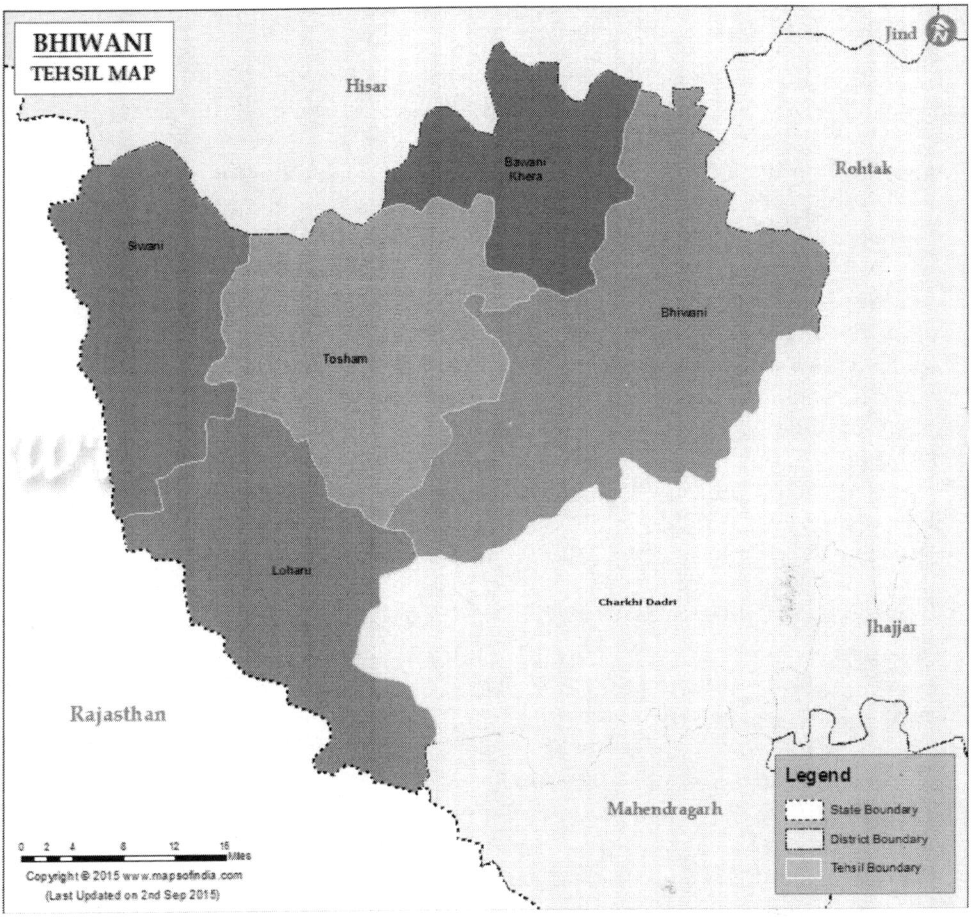

Figure 3.3: Map of Bhiwani District.

The Groundwater is mainly saline with some of small pocket of fresh water in Southwest. The groundwater level of the district is decreasing very fast. Lack of any Drainage system is the main cause of salinity of ground water. Total area covered by Bhiwani District is 5,099 sq. km. Temperature in the Bhiwani District varies from 2° C to 45° C. Rainfall is scanty (Annual Rainfall-483mm) mainly in months of July-August. Vegetation mainly thorny trees like Babool, Jandi, Kair, along with Neem, Sheesham, Peepal *etc.* Crops like Bajra and Cotton in *Kharif* and Wheat, Mustard in Rabi. According to the 2011 census Bhiwani district has a population of 1,629,109 roughly equal to the nation of Guinea-Bissauor the US state of Idaho. This gives it a ranking of 306th in India (out of a total of 640).The district has a population density of 341 inhabitants per square kilometre (880/sq mi). Its population growth rate over the decade 2001–2011 was 14.32 per cent. Bhiwani has a sex ratio of 884 females for every 1000 males, and a literacy rate of 76.7 per cent. The Bhiwani district also observed as emerging district in production of strawberry where the area under strawberry was 36 ha with a production of 650 ton.

3.4 Block: Hisar-1, Haryana

Hisar-1 is a block placed in Hisar district in Haryana. Placed in urban part of Haryana, it is one of the 9 blocks of Hisar district. According to the administration records, the block code of Hisar-1 is 70. The block has 45 villages and there are total 39725 houses in this block. As per Census 2011, the total population in Hisar-1 block is 204446. Out of this, 108802 are males 95644 are females. This block has 25642 children in the age bracket of 0-6 years. Out of this 13767 are boys and 11875 are girls. Literacy ratio in Hisar-1 block is 62 per cent. 127142 out of total 204446 populations are literate. The literacy rate of male is 70 per cent as 77143 males out of total 108802 are educated whereas female literacy rate is 52 per cent as 49999 out of total 95644 females are literate in this Block. The dark part is that illiteracy rate of Hisar-1 block is 37 per cent. It is to be mentioned that 77304 out of total 204446 persons are illiterate in this block. Male illiteracy rate is 29 per cent as 31659 males out of total 108802 are uneducated. Among the females the illiteracy ratio is 47 per cent and 45645 out of total 95644 females are illiterate. As per the secondary data 79071 persons are occupied while 125375 are non-working. Out of 79071 working people 25988 individuals are totally dependent on cultivation.

3.5 Block: Siwani, Haryana

Siwani is a block situated in Bhiwani district in Haryana. It is one among the 7 blocks of Bhiwani district and it is placed in rural part of Haryana. As per the administration register, the block number of Siwani is 79. The block has 36 villages and there are total 16709 houses in this block. As per census 2011, the total population in Siwani is 89240. Out of this, 47063 are males and 42177 are females. This block has 11944 children in the age group of 0-6 years. Out of this 6292 are boys and 5652 are girls. Literacy rate in Siwani block is 59 per cent. Out of total 89240 populations, 53374 is educated. The male literacy ratio is 69 per cent *i.e.*, 32923 males out of total 47063 are educated.

However female literacy rate is 48 per cent *i.e.*, 20451 out of total 42177 females are educated in this block. It may be mentioned that the illiteracy ratio of Siwani block is very low (40 per cent). Out of total 89240 populations, 35866 persons are illiterate. Male illiteracy ratio is 30 per cent *i.e.* 14140 males out of total 47063 are uneducated. Similarly, the females the illiteracy ratio is 51 per cent *i.e.*, 21726 out of total 42177 females are illiterate in this block. The total number of employed persons in Siwani block is 42619 while 46621 are unemployed. Out of 42619 working people 17812 persons are totally dependent on agriculture.

3.6 Socio-economic Characteristics of Strawberry Growers

3.6.1 Educational Status of the Strawberry Growers

Modern agricultural practices are increasingly turning out to be knowledge based and the need of education for many of rural farmers are required for gaining expertise on the specific field knowledge. Educated farmers are early innovators and adopters. It is copied by those with less schooling. Hence, education became an important parameter for every farm family. The overall education status of

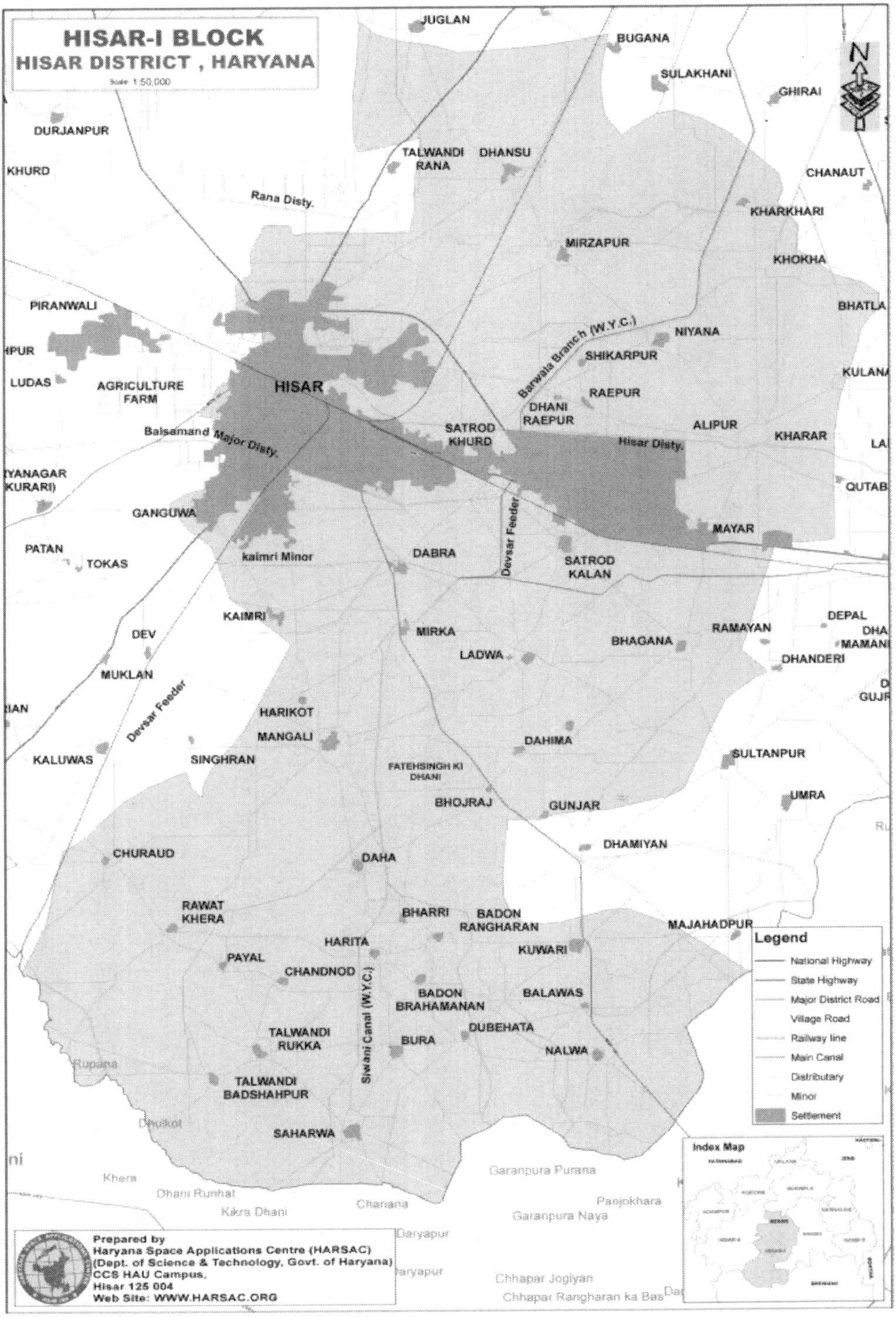

Figure 3.4: Map of Hisar-I Block.

Figure 3.5: Map of Siwani Block.

the strawberry growers was found to be very satisfactory.Keeping this in view, educational status of the farmers of the sample household for different categories of farm had been analysed and presented in Table 3.3. Only 9.16 strawberry growers were illiterate in the study area. If we see the standard basis formal education then highest share was estimated to be for in high school (36.67 per cent) followed by graduate (20 per cent), senior secondary education (12.50 per cent), primary (15 per cent) and Post Graduate (6.67 per cent).

Similarly, the category wise analysis of education status shows that High school education was having the highest share among the all standards of education in all the categories. The graduation education shared next highest in the category of small (20.63 per cent) and large (33.33 per cent) whereas primary (21.21 per cent) in category of medium as second highest share among the education standards in the study area. The third largest share in small category was primary (14.29 per cent), whereas primary and post graduate both education standards equally shared in category of large (8.33 per cent) at third place but in category of medium the higher secondary and illiterate were equally (18.18 per cent) distributed and shared as third highest education standard among the strawberry growers in study area Table 3.3. Therefore, it very apparent from the study that the more than 90 per cent of the

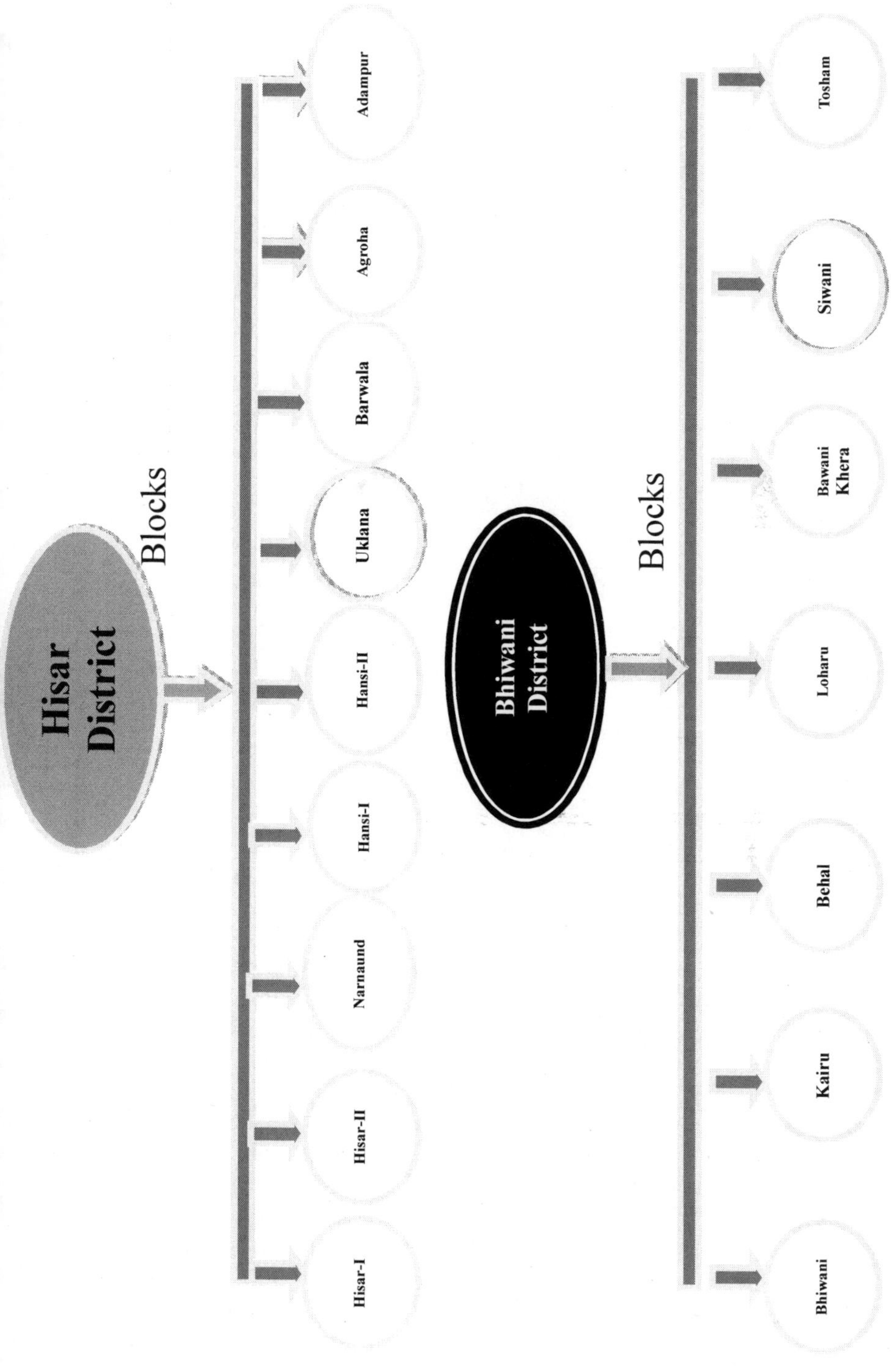

Figure 3.6: Block in Hisar and Bhiwani Districts.

respondents were well educated and adopted the strawberry cultivation. Hence, the adoption of high value crops and education are very much co-related.

Hence, increasing literacy of strawberry grower is a major concern and it must be taken up by the state government.

Table 3.3: Educational Status of the Strawberry Growers

Educational Level	*Number of Family Members by Size of Holding*			
	Small	*Medium*	*Large*	*Overall*
Illiterate	8 (07.62)	10 (18.18)	-	18 (09.00)
Primary	15 (14.28)	12 (21.82)	3 (07.50)	30 (15.00)
High school	40 (38.10)	15 (27.27)	18 (45.00)	73 (36.50)
Higher secondary school	13 (12.38)	10 (18.18)	2 (05.00)	25 (12.50)
Graduate	22 (20.95)	5 (09.10)	13 (32.50)	40 (20.00)
Post Graduate	7 (06.67)	3 (05.45)	4 (10.00)	14 (07.00)
Total	**105** **(100.00)**	**55** **(100.00)**	**40** **(100.00)**	**200** **(100.00)**

Note: Figure in the parentheses are percentage to the total.

3.6.2 Family Size of the Strawberry Growers

The average size of small category of strawberry grower in the study area was reported to be 6.08 number of family members in which adult male contributed 32.07 per cent and followed by adult female (29.44 per cent), child male (19.57 per cent) and child female (18.91 per cent). The size of family under medium category of strawberry grower found to be 5.75 numbers of family members. Among these members major share was accounted as adult male (31.65 per cent) and followed by adult female (29.57 per cent), child male (22.26 per cent) and child female (16.52 per cent). Similarly, the family size of large category of strawberry grower was reported as 5.74 numbers of family members, among the members adult male accounted to be 32.75 per cent which is followed by adult female (25.44 per cent), child male (22.47 per cent) and child female (19.34 per cent). The overall, family size across the category was observed to be 5.90 numbers of members in a family in which adult male observed the higher share of 32.20 per cent followed by female (28.81 per cent), child male (20.85 per cent) and child female (18.14 per cent). Hence, from the above discussion it is concluded that the size of family was more or less same on all three categories of farmers. Which ranges between 5 to 7 members but in overall the size of a family is 5.90 numbers of family members (Table 3.4).

Table 3.4: Family Size of the Strawberry Growers

Age Group	*Number of Family Members*			
	Small	*Medium*	*Large*	*Overall*
Adult male	1.95 (32.07)	1.82 (31.65)	1.88 (32.75)	1.90 (32.20)
Adult female	1.79 (29.44)	1.70 (29.57)	1.46 (25.44)	1.70 (28.81)
Child male	1.19 (19.57)	1.28 (22.26)	1.29 (22.47)	1.23 (20.85)
Child female	1.15 (18.91)	0.95 (16.52)	1.11 (19.34)	1.07 (18.14)
Total	**6.08 (100)**	**5.75 (100)**	**5.74 (100)**	**5.90 (100)**
Average age (years)	**50.98**	**52.30**	**49.50**	**51.05**

Note: i) Figures in parentheses are percentage to the total, ii) Adult $\geq$ 18 years and Child < 18 years.

Table 3.5: Distribution of the Family Member of Strawberry Growers by Occupation

Occupation	*Occupation of the Family Member of the Respondent by Size of Holding*			
	Small	*Medium*	*Large*	*Overall*
Agriculture	1.97 (24.26)	1.90 (23.37)	1.74 (22.39)	1.90 (23.60)
Livestock	1.00 (12.32)	1.00 (12.30)	1.00 (12.87)	1.00 (12.42)
Service	1.15 (14.16)	1.36 (16.73)	1.11 (14.29)	1.20 (14.91)
Business	1.00 (12.32)	1.00 (12.30)	1.00 (12.87)	1.00 (12.42)
Household	1.24 (15.27)	1.20 (14.76)	1.33 (17.12)	1.25 (15.53)
Education	1.76 (21.67)	1.67 (20.54)	1.59 (20.46)	1.70 (21.12)
Total	**8.12 (100)**	**8.13 (100)**	**7.77 (100)**	**8.05 (100)**

Note: Figures in parentheses are percentage to the total.

3.6.3 Occupation of the Family Member of the Strawberry Growers

The occupation of the family member in the study area of strawberry growers has been presented in the Table 3.5. It is evident from the that 23.60 per cent of the strawberry growers across the categories was found to be engaged in agriculture, of which small category (24.26 per cent) contributed maximum share which was followed by medium (23.37 per cent) and large (22.39 per cent) categories of farm (Table 3.5). members of the large category engaged in livestock (12.87 per cent) contributed maximum share which was followed by small (12.32 per cent) and medium (12.30 per cent) categories of farm. Majority of medium (16.73 per cent) and large (14.29 per cent) categories were in services than the small (14.16 per cent) category, of which the overall was found to be about 15 per cent contributed by service in the study area.

Further, it was observed that more or less of family member of strawberry grower across the categories are found to be engaged in business of which 12.87 per cent contributed bylarge and followed by small (12.32 per cent) and medium (12.30 per cent) categories of strawberry grower. Overall, 12.42 per cent of the family members were found to be engaged in business across the categories. In occupation of household 15.53 per cent of family members were found to be engaged across the categories of farms. In household maximum contribution of 17.12 per cent by large and followed by small (15.27 per cent) and medium (14.76 per cent) categories of strawberry grower. The average contribution of school was found to be 21.12 per cent across the categories, of which 21.67 per cent was contributed by the small category and slightly followed by the medium (20.54 per cent) and large (20.46 per cent) categories of family of strawberry grower. From the above discussion it can be concluded that majority of the family members of the strawberry grower were engaged in agriculture as an occupation and agriculture is recognized as major occupation of the state.

3.6.4 Land Holding Size of the Strawberry Growers

The size of land holding of a farmer in the society is good indicator of the prosperity of the farmer. The larger the size of land holding farmers is recognized prosperous one. On an average the size of land holding reported as 2.39 ha, 3.89 ha and 4.65 ha of small, medium and large strawberry growers. The overall size of cultivable land was 3.25 ha in the study area. It is very clear from the analysis that size of land holding found to be increased with the increase in the size of category of

Table 3.6: Size of Land Holding of the Strawberry Growers

Land Particulars	*Size of Land Holding (in ha)*			
	Small	*Medium*	*Large*	*Overall*
Own	1.86 (14.33)	2.70 (18.99)	3.51 (22.96)	2.43 (18.07)
Leased-in	1.21 (35.18)	1.60 (31.58)	1.85 (35.19)	1.48 (33.59)
Leased-out	0.67 (23.78)	0.59 (28.38)	0.87 (23.70)	0.75 (25.70)
Total Cultivated Land	**2.41** **(100.00)**	**3.89** **(100.00)**	**4.65** **(100.00)**	**3.27** **(100.00)**

Note: Figures in parentheses are percentage to the total.

strawberry grower. The share of leased-in land has been observed from 32 per cent to 35 per cent of the total land of the respective category. Similar share (33.59 per cent) was also observed as an overall across the categories of the farmer (Table 3.6).

3.6.5 Status of Irrigation Facilities of the Strawberry Growers

The main source of irrigation was observed as canal in the study area for Kharif and Rabi season across the category. The secondary source of irrigation was STD/DTW. During kharif season irrigation sources were reported as canal, STD/DTW only. Whereas, during Rabi season the irrigation sources were canal, STW/DTW and water tank. It shows that farmers in the study area during the water harvesting during rainy season for irrigation in Rabi season through water tank. Even the water tank irrigation was observed during summer season also (Table 3.7).

Table 3.7: Area under different Sources of Irrigation of the Respondents

Season	*Irrigation Facilities*	*Irrigated Area (in ha)*			
		Small	*Medium*	*Large*	*Overall*
Kharif	Canal	1.96 (41.97)	3.01 (41.72)	4.10 (43.91)	2.68 (42.46)
	STW/DTW	2.09 (44.66)	3.47 (48.20)	4.17 (44.63)	2.89 (45.76)
	Rain fed	0.63 (13.37)	0.73 (10.08)	1.07 (11.46)	0.75 (11.78)
Sub Total		**4.48 (100.00)**	**7.21 (100.00)**	**9.34 (100.00)**	**6.32 (100.00)**
Rabi	Canal	1.96 (37.75)	3.01 (36.84)	4.10 (39.99)	2.68 (37.27)
	STW/DTW	2.08 (40.18)	3.47 (42.55)	4.17 (40.64)	2.89 (4016)
	Water Tank	0.48 (9.14)	0.87 (10.62)	1.16 (11.35)	0.87 (12.11)
	Rain fed	0.67 (12.93)	0.82 (9.99)	0.82 (8.03)	0.75 (10.46)
Sub Total		**5.19 (100.00)**	**8.16 (100.00)**	**10.25 (100.00)**	**7.20 (100.00)**
Summer	STW/DTW	0.65 (41.18)	0.83 (47.74)	1.33 (50.46)	0.84 (44.06)
	Water Tank	0.93 (58.82)	0.91 (52.26)	1.31 (49.54)	1.06 (55.94)
Sub Total		**1.58 (100.00)**	**1.74 (100.00)**	**2.64 (100.00)**	**1.90 (100.00)**
Total		**11.25**	**17.11**	**22.23**	**15.42**

Note: Figures in parentheses are percentage to the total.

3.6.6 Cropping Pattern of the Strawberry Growers

The cropping pattern of farmers of Haryana is mainly in two seasons *i.e.* Rabi and Kharif. The analysis of cropping pattern shows that the average area cultivated by farmers in the state was estimated 8.80 ha across the categories of growers. Out of total cultivable area under Rabi it was estimated at 3.93 ha and 4.12 ha during Kharif season. The area under summer season was found to be negligible (0.75 ha). The larger share of area was observed to be higher during Kharif season due to rains as mostly crops were rain fed in nature. The major crops during Rabi season were wheat, mustard, gram and strawberry across the category in the study area. Similar trends of area under crops were reported on small, medium and large categories of farmer.

In Kharif season major crops were cotton, guar, bajra across the category of farmer. Similar trend of area under crops was observed on individual category of the farmer. Only single crops was reported in the season of summer *i.e.* cucurbits. The cropping intensity has been worked out 205 per cent, 216.14 per cent and 217.97 per cent for small, medium and large category of farmers, respectively. The cropping intensity was found to be increased with the increase in size of the category of the farmer in the study area. The overall cropping intensity has been worked out to be of 213.59 per cent (Table 3.8).

Table 3.8: Cropping Pattern of the Respondents

Season	*Crop*	*Area under Different Crops (in ha)*			
		Small	*Medium*	*Large*	*Overall*
Rabi	Strawberry	0.44 (14.33)	0.83 (18.99)	1.24 (22.96)	0.71 (18.07)
	Wheat	1.08 (35.18)	1.38 (31.58)	1.90 (35.19)	1.32 (33.59)
	Mustard	0.73 (23.78)	1.24 (28.38)	1.28 (23.70)	1.01 (25.70)
	Gram	0.67 (21.82)	0.76 (17.39)	0.82 (15.19)	0.74 (18.83)
	Green Fodder (Rabi)	0.15 (4.89)	0.16 (3.66)	0.16 (2.96)	0.15 (3.82)
Sub Total		**3.07 (100.00)**	**4.37 (100.00)**	**5.40 (100.00)**	**3.93 (100.00)**
Kharif	Cotton	1.47 (42.16)	2.27 (21.59)	2.69 (47.86)	1.94 (47.09)
	Guar	0.75 (21.74)	0.87 (19.77)	1.09 (19.40)	0.85 (20.63)
	Moong	0.46 (13.33)	0.35 (7.95)	0.47 (8.36)	0.41 (9.95)

Season	*Crop*	*Area under Different Crops (in ha)*			
		Small	*Medium*	*Large*	*Overall*
	Bajra	0.61 (17.68)	0.73 (16.59)	1.22 (21.71)	0.76 (18.45)
	Green Fodder (Kharif)	0.16 (4.64)	0.18 (4.09)	0.15 (2.67)	0.16 (3.88)
Sub Total		**3.45 (100)**	**4.40 (100)**	**5.62 (100)**	**4.12 (100)**
Summer	Cucurbits	0.56 (100.00)	0.74 (100.00)	1.23 (100.00)	0.75 (100.00)
Total		**7.08**	**9.51**	**12.25**	**08.80**
Cropping Intensity (per cent)		205.00	216.44	217.97	**213.59**

Note: Figures in parentheses are percentage to the total.

3.6.7 Productivity of different Crops of the Strawberry Growers

The productivity of various crops grown in season of Rabi, Kharif and Summer in the study area is presented in Table 3.9. The state Haryana has been recognized for high productivity of crops grown in the state. The high productivity of crops occurs due to better management and adoption of modern technology in the study area.

Table 3.9: Productivity of different Crops of the Respondents

Season	*Crop*	*Productivity of different crops (qt/ha)*			
		Small	*Medium*	*Large*	*Overall*
Rabi	Strawberry	256.27	246.52	246.88	253.68
	Wheat	45.16	43.45	45.11	45.15
	Mustard	18.38	18.73	17.62	18.16
	Gram	14.85	14.06	13.90	14.49
	Green Fodder (*Rabi*)	1348.75	1325.50	1314.06	1333.33
Kharif	Cotton	20.11	19.53	19.22	19.86
	Guar	14.86	16.67	15.89	15.13
	Moong	16.06	17.50	19.17	16.64
	Bajra	18.46	17.99	20.13	18.95
	Green Fodder (Kharif)	1361.11	1325.50	1532.89	1449.32
Summer	Cucurbits	717.26 (717.26)	716.29 (716.29)	807.29 (807.29)	742.10 (20.62)

Chapter 4

Results and Discussion

In this chapter, the facts and findings of this study along with the discussion have been presented under the following sub-sections.

- ☆ Economics of production of strawberry
- ☆ Process of marketing of strawberry
- ☆ Marketing costs, margins and price spread in strawberry
- ☆ Problems faced by the producers/traders in production/marketing of strawberry

4.1 Economics of Production of Strawberry

Theoretically production can be defined as a process of combining various material and immaterial inputs in order to make something for consumption *i.e.* the output. It is the act of creating output, a good or service which has value and contributes to the utility of individuals. Since the primary purpose of economic activity is to produce utility for individuals, it is measured as production during a time period of all activities which either creates utility during the period or which increases ability of the society to create utility in the future.Production of a commodity or service requires the use of certain resources or factors of production. Since most of the resources necessary to carry on production are scarce relative to demand for them they are called economic resources. Resources, which are called as factors of production, are combined in various ways, by farms or enterprises, to produce an annual flow of goods and services. Effort has been made in this section to examine the economics of production of strawberry by applying various farm management concepts.

It may be noted that fruit crops being perishable in nature, the strawberry orchard should preferably be located at a place where transportation to the market is easy and economical. Further, the cultivation of strawberry need a fertile soil and it necessitates proper selection of site. The rental value of land in Hisar and Bhiwani districts, on an average has been found to be ₹ 57020 per hectare per annum.

4.1.1 Establishment Cost of Strawberry Orchard

The establishment cost of strawberry cultivation is presented in Table 4.1. The initial cost (establishment cost) of cultivation consists of land drip irrigation, permanent fencing, and low tunnel. The Table 4.1 evident that the total cost of establishment of strawberry orchard per ha was observed to be highest in small category of orchard which was followed by medium and large category with the amount of ₹ 153.93 thousand, ₹ 145.18 thousand and ₹ 144.08 thousand per ha, respectively. Overall, it was estimated ₹ 149.55 thousand per ha across the categories. The cost incurred for strawberry required adequate water for its better growth and production, therefore irrigation facilities was required to meet the water requirement for the crop hence, the cost incurred on drip irrigation was estimated to be 46.82 per cent of total cost in small category, followed by medium (42.99 per cent) and large (38.40 per cent) category of farms.

Table 4.1: Establishment Cost of Strawberry Growers by Size of Holdings

Particulars	*Establishment Cost of Strawberry (₹ in thousand/ha)*			
	Small	*Medium*	*Large*	*Overall*
Drip irrigation	72.08 (46.82)	61.40 (42.29)	55.33 (38.40)	65.79 (43.99)
Permanent fencing	36.80 (23.91)	37.55 (25.87)	39.13 (27.16)	37.47 (25.06)
Low tunnel	45.05 (29.27)	46.23 (31.84)	49.63 (34.44)	46.29 (30.95)
Total cost	**153.93 (100.00)**	**145.18 (100.00)**	**144.08 (100.00)**	**149.55 (100.00)**

Note: Figures in parentheses are percentage to the total.

Source: Field Survey (2015-16).

The fencing is also required for protection of strawberry orchard from Nilgai (Blue Bull) and Chital like wild animals which are exists in large numbers in the study area. The cost incurred for fencing was estimated highest on large farms and followed by medium and small category of farms and it contributed 27.16 per cent, 25.87 per cent and 23.91 per cent of the total establishment cost respectively. In this part of the country, generally temperature remains more than 30°C during the month of September to October *i.e.* sowing time of strawberry, and remains lower less than 3° C during the month of December and January, both the extreme weather condition leads to serious damage to the crop, therefore, farmers' use plastic sheets as low tunnel to protect their crop from abrupt weather conditions. However, the costs incurred for low tunnel for various categories have been contributed 34.44 per cent on large farms, followed by medium (31.84 per cent) and small (29.27 per cent) category of farms. Similarly, per hectare overall establishment cost across the different farm categories was estimated 43.99 per cent on drip irrigation, 30.95 per cent on low tunnel and 25.06 per cent contributed as cost of permanent fencing.

From the discussion it may be concluded that the category wise establishment cost was found to be highest on small category farms followed by medium and large category of farms, hence, large share of investment was observed on drip irrigation across the various category of farms. The drip irrigation is pivot component of establishment cost to start the strawberry cultivation.

4.1.2 Operational Cost of Strawberry Orchard

Strawberry is a seasonal crop and required cost to perform petty operations time to time. The operational cost of strawberry cultivation includes cost of preparation of land, bed preparation, manure, hired labour, runners, replacement cost, fertilizers with growth regulator, irrigation, plant protection, picking and miscellaneous charges are presented in Table 4.2. The total operational cost in case of small category of farms was accounted to be ₹ 670.35 thousand per ha in which the major cost incurred on runners and it accounted to be 47.65 per cent of the total cost. Second major cost was observed plant protection *i.e.* 13.16 per cent followed by cost incurred on hired human (10.84 per cent), costs of manure (5.01 per cent), replacement cost (4.69 per cent), irrigation (3.78 per cent), fertilizers costs (3.62 per cent), picking (2.39 per cent), preparation of land (0.95 per cent), and bed preparation (0.28 per cent).

Table 4.2: Operational Cost of Strawberry Orchard

Particulars	*Category of Strawberry Grower (₹ in thousand/ha)*			
	Small	*Medium*	*Large*	*Total Cost*
Land preparation	6.36 (0.95)	5.70 (0.77)	4.97 (0.63)	5.90 (0.83)
Bed preparation	1.88 (0.28)	1.79 (0.24)	1.70 (0.21)	1.82 (0.26)
Manure	33.58 (5.01)	31.26 (4.23)	24.01 (3.03)	31.03 (4.35)
Hired labour	72.69 (10.84)	134.78 (18.22)	194.99 (24.64)	114.23 (16.01)
Runners	319.45 (47.65)	324.71 (43.89)	327.54 (41.39)	322.51 (45.19)
Replacement cost	31.45 (4.69)	31.69 (4.28)	32.92 (4.16)	31.81 (4.46)
Urea	2.14 (0.32)	2.19 (0.30)	2.24 (0.28)	2.17 (0.30)
DAP	8.08 (1.21)	9.15 (1.24)	10.07 (1.27)	8.77 (1.23)
MOP	2.07 (0.31)	2.20 (0.30)	2.26 (0.29)	2.14 (0.30)

Particulars	Category of Strawberry Grower (₹ in thousand/ha)			
	Small	*Medium*	*Large*	*Total Cost*
Zinc	4.87 (0.73)	5.30 (0.72)	5.98 (0.76)	5.21 (0.73)
Sulphur	1.30 (0.19)	1.24 (0.17)	1.29 (0.16)	1.28 (0.18)
Growth regulator	5.79 (0.86)	5.95 (0.80)	7.77 (0.98)	6.23 (0.87)
Total Chemical Costs	**24.25** **(3.62)**	**26.03** **(3.52)**	**29.61** **(3.74)**	**25.81** **(3.62)**
Irrigation	25.31 (3.78)	25.78 (3.48)	23.57 (2.98)	25.09 (3.52)
Plant protection cost	88.21 (13.16)	85.78 (11.60)	76.57 (9.67)	85.21 (11.94)
Picking	16.00 (2.39)	15.68 (2.12)	14.99 (1.89)	15.71 (2.20)
Depreciation	19.26 (2.87)	21.34 (2.89)	22.89 (2.89)	20.56 (2.88)
Sub Total	**638.44** **(95.24)**	**704.54** **(95.24)**	**753.76** **(95.24)**	**679.67** **(95.24)**
Interest on working capital	31.91 (4.76)	35.21 (4.76)	37.67 (4.76)	33.97 (4.76)
Total	**670.35** **(100.00)**	**739.76** **(100.00)**	**791.43** **(100.00)**	**713.64** **(100.00)**

Note: Figure in the parentheses are percentage to the total.

Source: Field Survey (2015-16).

On medium category of farms, the total operational cost was worked out to be ₹ 739.76 thousand per ha in which the major share contributed by cost of runners (43.89 per cent), followed by hired human labour (18.22 per cent), plant protection (11.60 per cent), replacement cost (4.28 per cent), manure (4.23 per cent), fertilizers costs (3.52 per cent), irrigation (3.48 per cent) picking (2.12 per cent), preparation of land (0.77 per cent), and bed preparation (0.24 per cent). Similarly, the total operation cost in case of large category of farms was estimated to be ₹ 791.43 thousand per ha. Among the total operational cost the major cost was found on runners (41.39 per cent) followed by hired human labour (24.64 per cent), plant protection (9.67 per cent), replacement cost (4.16 per cent), fertilizers costs (3.74 per cent), manure (3.03 per cent), irrigation (2.98 per cent), picking (1.89 per cent), preparation of land (0.63 per cent), and bed preparation (0.21 per cent).Overall, the total operational cost, across the different categories of farms was estimated to be ₹ 713.64 thousand per ha revealed that the overall highest operational cost accounted to be 45.19 per cent on runners followed by hired human labour (16.01 per cent), plant protection

(11.94 per cent), replacement cost (4.46 per cent),manure (4.35 per cent),fertilizers costs (3.62 per cent),irrigation (3.52 per cent), picking (2.20 per cent), preparation of land (0.83 per cent) and bed preparation (0.26 per cent) in the study area.

Hence, it reveals from the findings that a major share of investment in operational cost was found to be on runners among the various components of operational cost as the runners were purchased from outside the state (Himachal Pradesh) which involved a high cost. Therefore, the capacity building of farmer in reproduction of runners is required to reduce the cost.

4.1.3 Cost on Marketing of Strawberry at the Producers' Level

Strawberry is a highly perishable fruits and therefore, the marketing cost is a major component in strawberry cultivation. The marketing cost of strawberry includes cost of packing material, packing charges, transportation and unloading charges given by the producer' farmer which are presented in Table 4.3.

Table 4.3: Marketing Cost of Strawberry

Particulars	*Marketing Cost of Strawberry (₹ in thousand/ha)*			
	Small	*Medium*	*Large*	*Total Cost*
Packing material	192.50 (65.29)	179.62 (64.36)	167.38 (63.31)	183.93 (64.66)
Packing cost	15.24 (5.17)	15.58 (5.58)	16.15 (6.11)	15.52 (5.46)
Transportation	81.25 (27.56)	78.49 (28.12)	75.87 (28.70)	79.42 (27.92)
Unloading charges	5.87 (1.99)	5.41 (1.94)	4.98 (1.88)	5.57 (1.96)
Total	**294.86** **(100.00)**	**279.10** **(100.00)**	**264.38** **(100.00)**	**284.44** **(100.00)**

Note: Figure in the parentheses are percentage to the total.

Source: Field Survey (2015-16).

The marketing cost is maximum in case of small category of farms which was accounted to be ₹ 294.86 thousand per ha followed by medium *i.e.* ₹ 279.10 and large category of farms *i.e.* ₹ 264.38 per ha in which the major cost incurred on packing material and it accounted for 65.29, 64.36 and 63.31 per cent of total marketing cost on small, medium and large category of farms. Second major cost component was transportation cost. It was observed highest on large category of farms *i.e.* 28.70 per cent followed by medium (28.12 per cent) and small category of farms (27.56 per cent). Other marketing cost was packing cost incurred 6.11, 5.58, and 5.17 per cent of large, medium and small category of farms, respectively, whereas unloading charges was accounted 1.99 per cent on small, 1.94 per cent on medium and 1.88 per cent on large category of farms.

Overall, the total marketing cost, across the different categories of farms was estimated to be ₹ 284.44 thousand per ha in which highest marketing cost accounted to be 64.66 per cent on packing materials, followed by transportation (27.92 per cent), packing cost (5.46 per cent) and unloading charges (1.96 per cent) in the study area.

4.1.4 Cost of Cultivation of Strawberry

The total costs of strawberry cultivation including family labour per ha have been worked out to be ₹ 905.04 thousand, ₹ 947.65 thousand, ₹ 970.10 thousand on small, medium, large category of strawberry growers, respectively in which more than 91 per cent share contributed by variable cost on small, medium and 92 per cent share on large category of strawberry growers. The total cost found to be higher on large category of farms mainly due to more use of hired labour, runners, plastic mulching and fertilizers measures comparative to medium and small category of strawberry growers. Similarly, the cost of runners, hired labour, family labour and plant protection were found to be higher cost components in overall cost which shared 34.66 per cent, 12.28 per cent, 12.17 per cent and 9.16 per cent of overall total cost of strawberry cultivation *i.e.* ₹ 930.39 thousand per ha.

It may be concluded from the discussion that the total cost of strawberry cultivation including family labour as well as excluding family labour were found to be increased with the increase of strawberry orchard (Table 4.4).

4.1.5 Cost of Cultivation of Strawberry by different Cost Concepts

Per hectare cost of strawberry cultivation using cost concepts of various categories of strawberry growers is depicted in Table 4.5. It reveals from Table 4.5 that Cost A worked out to be ₹ 719.45 thousand, ₹ 792.19 thousand and ₹ 844.49 thousand per ha on small, medium and large categories of strawberry growers. The cost incurred on purchasing of runners, marketing cost and hired labour was the major components of Cost A on all categories of the strawberry growers in the study area. The overall Cost A was worked out to be ₹ 764.39 thousand per ha across the different categories of farms, in which 34.12 per cent of runners cost observed as the major cost component followed by hired labour (12.08 per cent) and plant protection (9.01 per cent). The Cost B on small, medium, large category of strawberry farms worked to be ₹ 785.30 thousand, ₹ 861.02 thousand and ₹ 912.34 thousand per ha, respectively.

Table 4.4: Cost of Cultivation of Strawberry in Hisar and Bhiwani, Haryana

Particulars	*Cost of Cultivation of Strawberry (₹ in thousand/ha)*			
	Small	*Medium*	*Large*	*Overall*
(A) Variable cost				
Land preparation	6.36 (0.70)	5.70 (0.60)	4.97 (0.51)	5.90 (0.63)
Bed preparation	1.88 (0.21)	1.79 (0.19)	1.70 (0.18)	1.82 (0.20)
Hired labour	72.69 (8.03)	134.78 (14.22)	194.99 (20.10)	114.23 (12.28)

Particulars	*Cost of Cultivation of Strawberry (₹ in thousand/ha)*			
	Small	*Medium*	*Large*	*Overall*
Family labour	132.55 (14.65)	102.85 (10.85)	76.89 (7.93)	113.25 (12.17)
Runners	319.45 (35.30)	324.71 (34.26)	327.54 (33.76)	322.51 (34.66)
Replacement cost	31.45 (3.47)	31.69 (3.34)	32.92 (3.39)	31.81 (3.42)
Manure	33.58 (3.71)	31.26 (3.30)	24.01 (2.48)	31.03 (3.34)
Irrigation	25.31 (2.80)	25.78 (2.72)	23.57 (2.43)	25.09 (2.70)
Fertilizers	24.25 (2.68)	26.03 (2.75)	29.61 (3.05)	25.80 (2.77)
Plant protection	88.31 (9.76)	85.78 (9.05)	76.57 (7.89)	85.21 (9.16)
Plastic mulching	37.78 (4.17)	41.50 (4.38)	42.53 (4.38)	39.75 (4.27)
Picking cost	16.00 (1.77)	15.68 (1.65)	14.99 (1.55)	15.71 (1.69)
Sub Total	**789.62** **(87.25)**	**827.55** **(87.33)**	**850.29** **(87.65)**	**812.11** **(87.29)**
Interest on working capitals (@ 10 per cent)	39.48 (4.36)	41.38 (4.36)	42.51 (4.36)	40.61 (4.36)
Total variable cost (TVC)	**829.10** **(91.61)**	**868.93** **(91.69)**	**829.80** **(92.03)**	**852.72** **(91.65)**
(B) Fixed cost				
Rental value of land	57.10 (6.31)	57.90 (6.11)	55.60 (5.73)	57.02 (6.13)
Depreciation	10.09 (1.11)	9.89 (1.04)	9.45 (0.97)	10.03 (1.08)
Interest on fixed capital (@ 8.75 per cent)	8.75 (0.97)	10.93 (1.15)	12.25 (1.26)	10.63 (1.14)
Total fixed cost (TFC)	**75.94** **(8.39)**	**78.72** **(8.31)**	**77.30** **(7.97)**	**77.68** **(8.35)**
Total cost including family labour (TVC+TFC)	905.04 (100.00)	947.65 (100.00)	970.10 (100.00)	930.39 (100.00)
Total cost excluding family labour (TVC+TFC-family labour)	772.49 (85.35)	844.80 (89.15)	893.21 (92.07)	**817.14** **(87.83)**

Note: Figures in parentheses are the percentage to the total cost including family labour (TVC+TFC).

Source: Field Survey (2015-16).

Table 4.5: Cost of Cultivation of Strawberry by different Cost Concepts in Hisar and Bhiwani Districts of Haryana

Particulars	*Cost of Cultivation of Strawberry by Cost Concepts (₹ in thousand/ha)*			
	Small	*Medium*	*Large*	*Overall*
Land preparation	6.36 (0.69)	5.70 (0.59)	4.97 (0.50)	5.90 (0.62)
Bed preparation	1.88 (0.20)	1.79 (0.19)	1.70 (0.17)	1.82 (0.19)
Hired labour	72.69 (7.92)	134.78 (13.98)	194.99 (19.71)	114.23 (12.08)
Cost of runners	319.45 (34.80)	324.71 (33.69)	327.54 (33.11)	322.51 (34.12)
Replacement cost	31.45 (3.43)	31.69 (3.29)	32.92 (3.33)	31.81 (3.37)
Manure	33.58 (3.66)	31.26 (3.24)	24.01 (2.43)	31.03 (3.28)
Irrigation	25.31 (2.76)	25.78 (2.67)	23.57 (2.38)	25.09 (2.65)
Fertilizers	24.25 (2.64)	26.03 (2.70)	29.61 (2.99)	25.80 (2.73)
Plant protection	88.31 (9.62)	85.78 (8.90)	76.57 (7.74)	85.21 (9.01)
Plastic mulching	37.78 (4.12)	41.50 (4.31)	42.53 (4.30)	39.75 (4.21)
Picking cost	16.00 (1.74)	15.68 (1.63)	14.99 (1.52)	15.71 (1.66)
Depreciation	28.14 (3.07)	29.78 (3.09)	30.90 (3.12)	29.15 (3.08)
Sub Total	**685.20 (74.65)**	**754.48 (78.28)**	**804.30 (81.31)**	**728.01 (77.01)**
Interest on working capital	34.25 (3.73)	37.71 (3.91)	40.20 (4.06)	36.39 (3.85)
Cost A	**719.45 (78.38)**	**792.19 (82.19)**	**844.49 (85.37)**	**764.39 (80.86)**
Rental Value of land	57.1 (6.22)	57.9 (6.01)	55.6 (5.62)	57.02 (6.03)
Interest on fixed capital	8.75 (0.95)	10.93 (1.13)	12.25 (1.24)	10.63 (1.12)
Cost B	**785.30 (85.56)**	**861.02 (89.33)**	**912.34 (92.23)**	**832.04 (88.02)**

Particulars	Cost of Cultivation of Strawberry by Cost Concepts (₹ in thousand/ha)			
	Small	Medium	Large	Overall
Family Labour	132.55 (14.44)	102.85 (10.67)	76.89 (7.77)	113.25 (11.98)
Cost C	**917.85** **(100.00)**	**963.87** **(100.00)**	**989.23** **(100.00)**	945.29 (100.00)

Note: Figures in parentheses are the percentage to Cost C.

Source: Field Survey (2015-16).

The overall cost of strawberry cultivation was worked out to be ₹ 832.04 thousand per ha across the different categories of strawberry growers. The Cost C have been worked out to be ₹ 989.23 thousand per ha on large category of strawberry growers which was observed as highest followed by medium (₹ 963.87 thousand per ha) and small (₹ 917.85 thousand per ha) category of strawberry growers. The overall cost of strawberry cultivation was estimated to be ₹ 945.29 thousand per ha across the different categories of strawberry growers. Hence, all these costs *i.e.* Cost A, Cost B and Cost C were found to be increased with the increase of size of the strawberry orchard in the study area.

4.1.6 Returns from Strawberry Cultivation

The yield of strawberry cultivation was estimated to be highest in case of small (16007.82kg/ha) category of strawberry growers followed by medium (15678.20kg/ha) and large (14992.74kg/ha) farms, whereas, the overall yield was worked out to be 15714.16 kg/ha in the study area (Table 4.6). The gross farm income was worked out to be ₹ 2109.03 thousand, ₹ 2120.48 thousand and ₹ 2101.98thousand on small, medium and large categories of strawberry growers, respectively. The overall gross income of strawberry growers was estimated to be ₹ 2111.98 thousand per ha. Whereas net return including the family labour was worked out to be higher on small (₹ 1191.18 thousand/ha) followed by medium (₹ 1156.61 thousand/ha) and large (₹ 1112.75 thousand/ha) categories of strawberry growers. Similarly, the net return excluding the family labour was worked out to be highest on small, followed by medium and large categories of strawberry growers which was accounted to be ₹ 1323.73 thousand, ₹ 1259.46 thousand and ₹ 1189.64 thousand per ha, respectively. The farm business income of small, medium and large categories of strawberry growers was worked out to be ₹ 1389.58 thousand, ₹ 1328.29 thousand and ₹ 1257.49 thousand per ha in the study area. The overall farm business income was estimated to be ₹ 1347.59 thousand per ha across the various categories of strawberry growers. The family labour income was worked out to be higher on small category of strawberry growers *i.e.*, ₹ 1323.73 thousand per hectarefollowed by medium (₹ 1259.46 thousand/ha.) and large (₹ 1189.64 thousand/ha.) categories of strawberry growers.

The overall family labour income was worked out to be ₹ 1279.94 thousand per ha across the different categories of strawberry growers. The farm investment income of strawberry growers was estimated to be highest on small category (₹ 1191.18 thousand/ha) followed by medium (₹ 1156.61 thousand/ha) and large (₹ 1112.75 thousand/ha) categories of strawberry growers. Overall the farm investment income from strawberry worked out to be ₹ 1166.69 thousand per ha across the different categories of farms. The Benefit Cost Ratio (BCR) over paid out cost A of strawberry cultivation over total cost was worked out to be higher on small category of strawberry growers (2.93) followed by medium (2.68) and large (2.49) categories of farms whereas the Benefit Cost Ratio over paid out cost B was worked out to be 2.69, 2.46 and 2.30 on small, medium and large categories of strawberry growers, respectively.

Table 4.6: Returns from Strawberry Cultivation in Hisar and Bhiwani Districts of Haryana

Particulars	*Returns from Strawberry Cultivation (₹ in thousand/ha)*			
	Small	*Medium*	*Large*	*Overall*
Production (kg/ha)	16007.82	15678.20	14992.74	15714.16
Gross income	2109.03	2120.48	2101.98	2111.98
Net return including family labour	1191.18	1156.61	1112.75	1166.69
Net return excluding family labour	1323.73	1259.46	1189.64	1279.94
Farm business income	1389.58	1328.29	1257.49	1347.59
Family labour income	1323.73	1259.46	1189.64	1279.94
Farm investment income	1191.18	1156.61	1112.75	1166.69
Cost of cultivation/kg	54.34	61.48	65.98	60.16
Benefit Cost ratio (BCR)				
i) Paid out cost (GFI/Cost A)	2.93	2.68	2.49	2.76
ii) Paid out cost (GFI/Cost B)	2.69	2.46	2.30	2.54
iii) Total cost (GFI/Cost C)	2.30	2.20	2.12	2.23

Source: Field Survey (2015-16).

Similarly, the Benefit Cost Ratio over paid out cost C was worked out to be higher on small category of strawberry growers (2.30) followed by medium (2.20) and large (2.12) categories of farms. All these facts indicate that strawberry cultivation is profitable in the study area.

Hence, from the discussion it can be concluded that the net returns from strawberry cultivation was observed to be increased with the decrease in the size of the strawberry farms it was due to higher yield on small category of farms compared to medium and large category of farms. It was found that strawberry cultivation in the area was profitable wherein the BCR found to be more than one (Table 4.6).

4.1.7 Firm Efficiency Analysis

Broadly, technical efficiency has been estimated frequently by two general approaches, parametric and non-parametric methods. The parametric approach uses econometric method, whereas a mathematical approach uses mathematical linear programming method is used in non-parametric mathematical approach. As a conventional practice, a number of parametric approaches have been extensively used to estimate input-output relationships in order to study the efficiency of resource allocation. However, these parametric approaches are often criticized on grounds of being unduly restrictive, heavily depending upon a number of assumptions, *etc.* Though both of these two approaches have some advantages and disadvantages over each other, the non-parametric approach, called the Data Envelopment Analysis (DEA), has become very popular among social science researchers as it does not require any a priory assumption about the form of the production function to be applied.

In this study we use the non-parametric DEA analysis to obtain the technical efficiency scores (under variable returns to scale) in measuring efficiency of the individual firms. We define efficiency as a measure of how efficiently the inputs are employed to achieve a given level of output. Inefficiency occurs owing to lack of managerial oversight of the production process. A farm is considered to be inefficient if it could produce the same output using fewer inputs (input oriented) or it could produce more output using same input (output oriented).

The Data Envelopment Analysis (DEA) is a linear (mathematical) programming based method first originated in the literature by Charnes, Cooper and Rhodes (1978) as a reformulation of the Farrell's (1957) single-output, single-input radial measure of technical efficiency to multiple-output, multiple-input case. Here, a concept of Relative Efficiency has been advanced. Accordingly, a DMU (Decision Making Unit) is to be rated as fully (100 percent) efficient on the basis of available evidence if and only if the performance of other DMUs does not show that some of its inputs or outputs can be improved without worsening some of its other inputs or outputs. This basic kind of efficiency is referred to as *'technical efficiency'* in economics.

Under this technique, for each of the n decision making units (DMU) which consume m different inputs to produce s different outputs, technical efficiency is given by the measure:

$$\sum_r u_r y_{rO} / \sum_i v_i x_{iO} \qquad \text{(Cooper, Seiford and Zhu, 2004)}$$

where,

y_{rO} = r^{th} output of a particular DMU, O;

x_{iO} = i^{th}output of a particular DMU, O;

u_r = Weight associated with each kind of output;

v_i = Weight associated with each kind of input.

The problem is to find these weights such that-

$$z = \sum_r u_r y_{rO} / \sum_i v_i x_{iO}$$

-*i.e.* the ratio of the virtual output to the virtual input of each DMU is maximized.

However, without additional constraints, this ratio would be unbounded. To deal with this, a set of normalizing constraints are introduced-

$$\sum_r u_r\, y_{rj} / \sum_i v_i\, x_{ij} \le 1$$

for $j = 1, 2, \ldots, n$; and

u_r *and* $v_i \ge 0$ for all i and r

which reflects the condition that virtual output to virtual input ratio of every DMU must be less than or equal to unity for non-negative weights.

The dual of this linear programming problem may be written in a transformed form as:

$$\theta^* = \min \theta$$

$$\text{Subject to } \sum_{j=1}^{n} x_{ij}\lambda_j \le \theta\, x_{iO} \qquad i = 1, 2, \ldots, m;$$

$$\sum_{j=1}^{n} y_{rj}\lambda_j \ge y_{rO} \qquad r = 1, 2, \ldots, s;$$

$$\lambda_j \ge 0 \qquad j = 1, 2, \ldots, n.$$

Table 4.7: Average Efficiency by different Categories of Strawberry Growers (in per cent)

Category of Farms	*Technical Efficiency*	*Allocative Efficiency*	*Cost Efficiency*
Small	83.20	67.10	57.00
Medium	89.30	80.80	72.20
Large	77.00	63.90	49.70
Overall	83.17	70.60	59.64

Source: DEA analysis of primary data.

Either the primal or the dual may be used to get an efficiency score for a particular farm since by virtue of the dual theorem $z^* = \theta^*$. We solve the dual problem to obtain the efficiency score for each of the farms. Since we can set $\theta = 1$ and $\lambda^*_k = 1$ with $\lambda^*_k = \lambda^*_O$ and all other $\lambda^*_j = 0$, a solution of dual always exists. This solution implies $\theta^* = 1$. DMUs for which $\theta^* < 1$ are inefficient while DMUs for which $\theta^* = 1$ are boundary points.

The efficiency scores obtained by DEA analysis can be summarized here by categorizing the efficiency scores obtained by the firms in Table 4.7. It is worthwhile to note that in this DEA analysis, as individual farms may not be operating at their optimum scale, we consider *Variable Returns to Scale (VRS)* in our *Output-Oriented* DEA model. Hence, the efficiency scores thus obtained essentially indicate *Pure Technical Efficiency (PTE)* of individual farms.

It is easy to find here that this *multi-input multi output* DEA analysis shows that the pure technical efficiency of the strawberry farms increase steadily with low holding size, which calls for newer wave of modernization drive in the higher size class in Haryana. In this multi-input multi-output model, the outputs are total production of strawberry. The inputs are fixed costs, variable costs, market incidentals (including depreciation) incurred by the firms.

4.2 Process of Marketing of Strawberry

4.2.1 Producers' Surplus of Strawberry

Marketed surplus of strawberry produced by different category of farms along and utilization pattern of strawberry is presented in Table 4.8.

Table 4.8: Marketed Surplus and Utilization Pattern of Strawberry

Particular	*Marketed Surplus of Strawberry (kg.)*			
	Small	*Medium*	*Large*	*Overall*
a) Family consumption	0.95 (0.006)	1.68 (0.011)	2.48 (0.017)	1.46 (0.009)
b) Social/Relative	0.65 (0.004)	1.05 (0.007)	1.47 (0.010)	0.92 (0.006)
c) Spoilage	1.82 (0.010)	2.55 (0.016)	3.45 (0.023)	2.35 (0.015)
d) Religious used	0.57 (0.004)	0.88 (0.006)	0.78 (0.005)	0.70 (0.004)
Total (a-d)	**3.99 (0.025)**	**6.16 (0.039)**	**8.18 (0.055)**	**5.43 (0.035)**
Marketable surplus	16003.83 (99.98)	15672.04 (99.96)	14984.56 (99.95)	15708.73 (99.97)
Marketed surplus	16003.83 (99.98)	15672.04 (99.96)	14984.56 (99.95)	**15708.73 (99.97)**

Note: Figures in the parentheses are percentage to the total.

Source: Field Survey (2015-16).

The marketable and marketed surplus of strawberry was found to be equal for all categories of farm. The requirement of strawberry for family consumption for different purposes was observed comparatively high on large (0.055 per cent) category of farms, followed by medium (0.039 per cent) and small (0.025 per cent) category of farms, whereas at overall level it was found to be 0.035 per cent of total produce. The retention capacity was observed more on large category of farms may be due to large size of family as compared to medium and small farms. The quantity retained in household across the different categories of farms was found to be 5.43 kg which was shared by quantity used for spoilage (0.015 per cent), as major share followed by family consumption (0.009 per cent), social obligation (0.006 per cent) and religious purpose (0.004 per cent). Hence, from the above discussion, it may be concluded that strawberry has its importance in spiritual/religious sphere too. The marketable and marketed surplus found to be equal because of its perishability (Table 4.8).

4.2.2 Disposal Pattern of Strawberry through different Marketing Channels

The existing disposal pattern of strawberry through different channel in the state is presented in Table 4.9. Four major marketing channels were identified for disposal off strawberry from the producers to the ultimate consumer which are discussed in the following paragraphs.

i) **Channel-I:** Producer → Wholesaler-cum-commission agent → Retailer → Consumer (46.42 per cent) Azadpur market (Delhi) and Hisar/Bhiwani;

ii) **Channel-II:** Producer → Wholesaler-cum-commission agent → Consumer (26.87 per cent) Azadpur market (Delhi) and Hisar/Bhiwani;

iii) **Channel-III:** Producer → Retailer → Consumer (17.73 per cent) (Hisar/Bhiwani); and

iv) **Channel-IV:** Producer → Consumer (8.99 per cent) (At Farm/Home).

Under channel-I, Strawberry disposed-off from producer to the ultimate consumers through wholesaler-cum-commission agent and retailer *i.e.*, Azadpur market (Delhi) and Hisar/Bhiwani. In channel-II, the wholesaler-cum-commission agent was found purchasing the produce from the growers and sell to the ultimate consumers. Whereas, in case of channel-III, it was found that the growers himself sell his produce to the retailers. In case of channel-IV, producer sales directly to the ultimate consumers at farm level or home.

Table 4.9: Disposal Pattern of Strawberry through different Marketing Channels

Marketing Channels	*Disposal Pattern of Strawberry (kg.)*			
	Small	*Medium*	*Large*	*Overall*
	Quantity Sold	*Quantity Sold*	*Quantity Sold*	*Quantity Sold*
Channel-I	6750.92 (42.18)	7757.54 (49.50)	8071.45 (53.87)	7291.85 (46.42)
Channel-II	3800.47 (23.75)	4508.52 (28.77)	4926.74 (32.88)	4220.44 (26.87)
Channel-III	3779.62 (23.62)	2155.92 (13.76)	1038.65 (6.93)	2784.91 (17.73)
Channel-IV	1672.82 (10.45)	1250.06 (7.98)	947.72 (6.32)	1411.54 (8.99)
Total	**16003.83 (100.00)**	**15672.04 (100.00)**	**14984.56 (100.00)**	**15708.73 (100.00)**

Note: Figures in the parentheses are percentage to the total.

Source: Field Survey (2015-16).

Hence, the preference to dispose-off the produce through different channels was the price offered to the produces. Table 4.9 depicts that on an average, 46.42 per cent of the produce was disposed-off through channel-I in which the highest share was found by large category (53.87 per cent), followed by medium (49.50 per cent) and small categories (42.18 per cent) of farms. Channel-I was found popular on large category of farms as compared to medium and small categories, through which they marketed their produce. Similarly, channel–II was most popular for large, medium and small category of strawberry growers through which they disposed-off 32.88 per cent, 28.77 per cent and 23.75 per cent of produce, respectively. At overall level, 26.87 per cent of the produce was disposed through channel-II. Under channel-III, small farmers disposed maximum of their produce and accounted 23.62 per cent to the total produce, followed by medium (13.76 per cent) and large (6.93 per cent) categories. At overall level, 17.73 per cent of the produce was disposed through channel-III in the selected market. In channel-IV direct sale was confined to the farmers. They sale maximum of their produce (10.45 per cent) through direct selling followed by medium (7.98 per cent) and large (6.32 per cent) category of farms. At overall level, 8.99 per cent of the produce was disposed through Channel-IV in the study area. Hence, it may be concluded that out of four channels, channels I and II were most popular in large category of farms and channel-III and IV were most popular in small category of farms (Table 4.9).

4.3 Marketing Costs, Margins and Price Spread in strawberry

4.3.1 Price Spread in Channel-I (Producer → Wholesaler-cum-commission Agent → Retailer → Consumer)

The finding regarding marketing margins and price spread in channel-I in Azadpur market Delhi, Hisar/Bhiwani and overall market is presented in Table4.10. In channel-I, in between the producer and ultimate consumer, there are two market intermediaries' *viz.*, wholesaler-cum-commission agent and retailer. The producer farmer hands over the produce to wholesaler-cum-commission agent, who sells the produce to the retailer and charges commission @ 8 per cent from the producer in Azadpur market Delhi. The costs of packaging, packing materials, unloading charges and transportation are borne by the producer. The average sale price of producer to wholesaler-cum-commission agent was ₹ 131.75 and ₹ 52.25 per kilogram in Azadpur (Delhi) and Hisar/Bhiwani markets, respectively. The overall sale price of these two markets is ₹ 92.00 per kilogram. It reveals that the net price received by the producer on an average is ₹ 100.96 per kilogram and ₹ 36.60 per kilogram in Azadpur (Delhi) and Hisar/Bhiwani markets, respectively and the average net price received by the producer in these two markets is ₹ 68.78 per kilogram which accounted for 47.23 per cent, 34.66 per cent and 40.95 per cent of consumer's price on Azadpur market (Delhi), Hisar/Bhiwani and overall basis, respectively. The major costs incurred by the producer in Azadpur market (Delhi) were cost of transportation, and commission @ 8 per cent and unloading charges which account for ₹ 7.15 per kilogram, ₹ 10.54 per kilogram and ₹ 0.50 per kilogram, respectively. Other costs *i.e.*, packaging materials and packaging were equal in both these markets which accounted for ₹ 12.00 per kilogram and ₹ 0.60 per kilogram. In case of Hisar/Bhiwani market, major cost incurred by the producer was transportation and unloading charges which accounted for ₹ 2.75 per kilogram and ₹ 0.30 per kilogram, while the packaging materials and packaging are found to be ₹ 12.00 per

Table 4.10: Price Spread in Marketing of Strawberry in Channel-I

Sl. No.	*Particulars*	*Price Spread in different Markets (₹ /kg)*		
		Delhi	*Hisar/Bhiwani*	*Overall*
1.	Net price received by producer	100.96 (47.23)	36.60 (34.66)	68.78 (40.95)
2.	Cost incurred by the producer			
i.	Packaging materials	12.00 (5.61)	12.00 (11.36)	12.00 (8.49)
ii.	Packaging charges	0.60 (0.28)	0.60 (0.57)	0.60 (0.42)
iii.	Transportation	7.15 (3.35)	2.75 (2.60)	4.95 (2.97)
iv.	Unloading charges	0.50 (0.23)	0.30 (0.28)	0.40 (0.26)
v.	Commission @8 per cent	10.54 (4.93)	-	7.36 (2.47)
	Sub-total (i to v)	**30.79 (14.40)**	**15.65 (14.82)**	**25.31 (14.61)**
3.	Sale price of producer/purchase price of wholesaler	131.75 (61.64)	52.25 (49.48)	92.00 (55.56)
4.	Net margin of wholesaler	28.75 (13.45)	13.35 (12.64)	21.05 (13.05)
5.	Sale price of wholesaler/purchase price of retailer	160.50 (75.09)	65.60 (62.12)	113.05 (68.60)
6.	Cost incurred by the retailer			
i.	Transportation	3.50 (1.64)	3.50 (3.31)	3.50 (2.48)
ii.	Loading and unloading charges	0.30 (0.14)	0.30 (0.28)	0.30 (0.21)
iii.	Spoilages	7.78 (3.64)	3.25 (3.08)	5.52 (3.36)
	Sub-total (i to iii)	**11.58 (5.42)**	**7.05 (6.68)**	**9.32 (6.05)**
7.	Net margin of retailer	41.67 (19.49)	32.95 (31.20)	37.31 (25.35)
8.	Sale price of retailer/purchase price of consumer	213.75 (100.00)	105.60 (100.00)	159.68 (100.00)

Note: Figures in the parentheses are percentage to the total.

Source: Field Survey (2015-16).

kilogram and ₹ 0.60 per kilogram, respectively which is same as Azadpur market (Delhi). It was observed that the cost of packaging and packaging materials was equal irrespective of market and marketing channels. The overall cost incurred by the producer in transportation, unloading and commission were ₹ 4.95, ₹ 0.40 and ₹ 7.36 per kilogram, respectively. The sale price of wholesaler-cum-commission agent to retailer was ₹ 160.50, ₹ 65.60 and ₹ 113.05 per kilogram, while their net margins were ₹ 28.75, ₹ 13.35 and ₹ 21.05 per kilogram in Azadpur market (Delhi), Hisar/Bhiwani and overall average, respectively. It was observed that wholesaler-cum-commission agent did not incur any cost during marketing process of strawberry. Finally retailer sold the produce to the ultimate consumer, during this process the marketing cost incurred by the retailer were ₹ 11.58 per kilogram in Azadpur market (Delhi), ₹ 7.05 per kilogram in Hisar/Bhiwani and ₹ 9.32 per kilogram in overall average which included the transportation, loading and unloading charges and spoilages charges. The sale price of retailers or purchase price of consumers was ₹ 213.75, ₹ 105.60 and ₹ 159.68 per kilogram and retailer's net margins were ₹ 41.67, ₹ 32.95 and ₹ 37.31per kilogram in Azadpur market (Delhi), Hisar/Bhiwani and overall average, respectively.

4.3.2 Price Spread in Channel-II (Producer → Wholesaler-cum-commission Agent → Consumer)

The marketing margins and price spread in channel-II in Azadpur market Delhi and Hisar/Bhiwani market are presented in Table 4.11.

Table 4.11: Price Spread in Marketing of Strawberry in Channel-II

Sl. No.	*Particulars*	*Price Spread in different Markets (₹/kg)*		
		Delhi	*Hisar/Bhiwani*	*Overall*
1.	Net price received by producer	100.96 (56.88)	38.60 (51.31)	69.78 (54.09)
2.	Cost incurred by the producer			
i.	Packaging materials	12.00 (6.76)	12.00 (15.95)	12.00 (11.35)
ii.	Packaging charges	0.60 (0.34)	0.60 (0.80)	0.60 (0.57)
iii.	Transportation	7.15 (4.03)	2.75 (3.65)	4.95 (3.84)
iv.	Unloading charges	0.50 (0.28)	0.30 (0.40)	0.40 (0.34)
v.	Commission @8 per cent	10.54 (5.94)	-	7.44 (5.89)
	Sub-total (i to v)	**30.79** **(17.35)**	**15.65** **(20.80)**	**23.22** **(19.07)**

Sl. No.	*Particulars*	*Price Spread in different Markets (₹/kg)*		
		Delhi	*Hisar/Bhiwani*	*Overall*
3.	Sale price of producer/purchase price of wholesaler	131.75 (74.23)	54.25 (72.09)	93.00 (73.16)
4.	Net margin of wholesaler	45.75 (25.77)	21.00 (27.91)	33.38 (26.84)
5.	Sale price of wholesaler/purchase price of consumer	177.50 (100.00)	75.25 (100.00)	126.38 (100.00)

Note: Figures in the parentheses are percentage to the total.

Source: Field Survey (2015-16).

In channel-II, in between the producer and ultimate consumer, there is only one market intermediary *viz.*, wholesaler-cum-commission agent. The producer farmer channelizes the produce to wholesaler-cum-commission agent and ultimately who sells the produce to the consumers. The costs of packaging materials, packaging, unloading charges and transportation are borne by the growers. Net price received by producer was ₹ 100.96, ₹ 38.60 in Azadpur market (Delhi) and Hisar/Bhiwani market, respectively and the overall net price received by producer was ₹ 69.78 per kilogram.

Accordingly the marketing cost incurred by the producer for these processes was ₹ 30.79, ₹ 15.65 in Azadpur market (Delhi) and Hisar/Bhiwani market, respectively and the overall marketing cost was found to be ₹ 23.22 per kilogram. The wholesaler-cum-commission agent channelizes the produce to the ultimate consumers at ₹ 177.50 and ₹ 75.25 per kilogram in Azadpur market (Delhi), Hisar/ Bhiwani markets, respectively. The overall price received by the wholesaler-cum-commission agent was found to be ₹ 126.38 per kilogram. The net margin of wholesaler-cum-commission agent was found to be ₹ 45.75 and ₹ 21.00 per kilogram in Azadpur market (Delhi), Hisar/Bhiwani market which constituted 25.77 and 27.91 per cent of the consumer's price whereas overall net margin was found to be ₹ 33.38 per kilogram which was 26.84 per cent of consumer's price. The results clearly show that producer's share in consumer's price was highest in Delhi if we ponder channel-II.

4.3.3 Price Spread in Channel-III (Producer → Retailer → Consumer)

Channel-III marketing channel was found in Hisar/Bhiwani markets only. There is only one marketing intermediary between the producer and ultimate consumer in this channel *viz.*, retailer. Table 4.12 represents the data that provides information on marketing margin and price spread in channel-III.

It reveals that producer received net price of ₹ 60.15 per kilogram which accounted for 58.68 per cent of consumer's price. Total marketing cost incurred by producer was ₹ 15.65 per kilogram. The costs of packaging materials, packaging, unloading charges and transportation are borne by the producers. The producer sold their produce to retailer at Hisar/Bhiwani market and received ₹ 75.80 per kilogram of strawberry. The retailer sold the produce to the ultimate consumers at the rate of ₹ 102.50 per kilogram and the net margin of retailer in Hisar/Bhiwani market was found to be ₹ 26.70 per kilogram. It was observed that retailer did not pay any cost during marketing process of strawberry in channel-III.

Table 4.12: Price Spread in Marketing of Strawberry in Channel-III

Sl.No.	*Particulars*	*Price Spread (₹/kg)*
		Hisar/Bhiwani
1.	Net price received by producer	60.15 (58.68)
2.	Cost incurred by the producer	
i.	Packaging materials	12.00 (11.71)
ii.	Packaging charges	0.60 (0.59)
iii.	Transportation	2.75 (2.68)
iv.	Unloading charges	0.30 (0.29)
	Sub-total (i to iv)	15.65 (15.27)
3.	Sale price of producer/purchase price of retailer	75.80 (73.95)
4.	Net margin of retailer	26.70 (26.05)
5.	Sale price of retailer/purchase price of consumer	102.50 (100.00)

Note: Figures in the parentheses are percentage to the total.

Source: Field Survey (2015-16).

4.3.4 Price Spread in Channel-IV (Producer → Consumer)

Channel-IV was the shortest marketing channel which was observed in strawberry marketing wherein there is no intermediary between producer and consumer. This channel was found only in case of farm gate/home of the producers. Table 4.13 represents the data which provides information on marketing margin and price spread in channel-IV. It reveals that producer had received a net price of ₹ 42.95 per kilogram which accounted for 77.32 per cent of consumer's price. Major costs incurred by the producer were packaging materials and packaging which amounted for ₹ 12.00 and ₹ 0.60 per kilogram, respectively. The sale price of strawberry in this channel was found to be ₹ 55.55 per kilogram.

Table 4.13: Price Spread in Marketing of Strawberry in Channel-IV

Sl.No.	*Particulars*	*Hisar/Bhiwani (₹ /kg)*
1.	Net price received by producer	42.95 (77.32)
2.	Cost incurred by the producer	
i.	Packaging materials	12.00 (21.60)
ii.	Packaging charges	0.60 (1.08)
	Sub-total (i to ii)	**12.60** **(22.68)**
3.	Sale price of producer/purchase price of consumer	55.55 (100.00)

Note: Figures in the parentheses are percentage to the total.

Source: Field Survey (2015-16).

Table 4.14: Channel-wise and Market-wise Price Spread of Strawberry

Particulars	*Price Spread of Strawberry by different Channels (₹/Kg.)*					
	Delhi Market		*Hisar/Bhiwani Markets*			*Local/Farm*
	I	*II*	*I*	*II*	*III*	*IV*
Net price received by the producer	100.96 (47.23)	100.96 (56.88)	36.60 (34.66)	38.60 (51.30)	60.15 (58.68)	42.95 (77.32)
Marketing cost	42.37 (19.82)	30.79 (17.35)	22.70 (21.50)	15.65 (20.80)	15.65 (15.27)	12.60 (22.68)
Marketing margin	70.42 (32.95)	45.75 (25.77)	46.30 (43.84)	21.00 (27.91)	26.70 (26.05)	0.00 (0.00)
Price spread	112.79 (52.77)	76.54 (43.12)	69.00 (65.34)	36.65 (48.70)	42.35 (41.32)	12.60 (22.68)
Consumer's price	213.75 (100.00)	177.50 (100.00)	105.60 (100.00)	75.25 (100.00)	102.50 (100.00)	55.55 (100.00)

Note: Figures in the parentheses are percentage to the total.

Source: Field Survey (2015-16).

Comparing the results, presented in Table 4.14 for different channel it was observed that producer's share in consumer's rupee was highest in direct sale in comparison to the channels where there are different intermediaries. In channels-I and II, net prices received by the producers was found to be 47.23 per cent and 56.88 per cent in Azadpur market (Delhi) and 34.66 per cent and 51.31 per cent of consumer's price in Hisar/Bhiwani market, respectively. Whereas in channels- III and IV the net price received by producer was per cent and 58.68 per cent and 77.32 per cent of consumer's price in Hisar/Bhiwani and Local market, respectively. This clearly shows that producer's share in consumer's rupee decreases with the increase in the number of intermediaries. However, the point should be noted here that volume of transaction is high through channels- I and II in Hisar/Bhiwani markets even the producer's share in consumer's rupee is high in channel-IV. This occurs because local market is unable to consume the total volume of production due to lack of local demand at the initial stage of production.

4.3.5 Marketing Efficiency

The marketing efficiency is essentially the degree of market performance (Acharya *et al.*, 1987). There are several approaches by which efficiency of the marketing system have been computed. There are some simple measures to assess the efficiency of the marketing system for agricultural commodities (Acharya *et al.*, 1987). Based on these measures the marketing efficiency of various channels in the study area was calculated and presented in Tables 4.10 to 4.13. Tables 4.10 to 4.13 show that the average selling price of producers was high in Channel-I and II (₹ 131.75/kg) in Azadpur market (Delhi) and followed by Channel-III (₹ 75.80/kg) in Hisar/Bhiwani market and in Channels-I and II (₹ 52.25/kg and ₹ 54.25/kg) in Hisar/Bhiwani market and Channel-IV (₹ 55.55/kg) at local/farm level. According to these, Channel-I and II at Azadpur market (Delhi) was rank first, Channel-III at Hisar/Bhiwani market was second, Channel-IV was rank third at local/farm level, and Channel-II and I at Hisar/Bhiwani market was rank fourth and fifth which depict that Channel-I and II at Azadpur market (Delhi) was more efficient compared to Channel-I, Channel-II, Channel-III at Hisar/Bhiwani market and Channel-IV at local/farm as because the producer's share in consumer's rupee is high in Channel-I and II (Tables 4.10 and 4.11) at Azadpur market (Delhi).

Table 4.15: Marketing Efficiency of Strawberry in Azadpur Market (Delhi)

Sl.No.	*Particulars*	*Unit*	*Channel-I*	*Channel-II*
1.	Consumer purchase price/Retailer sale price (RP)	(₹/kg)	213.75	177.50
2.	Total marketing cost (MC)	(₹/kg)	42.37	30.79
3.	Total net margins of intermediaries (MM)	(₹/kg)	70.42	45.75
4.	Net price received by producers (FP)	(₹/kg)	100.96	100.96
5.	Value added (1-4)	(₹/kg)	112.79	76.50
	Index of marketing efficiency			
A.	Acharya's method (MME) 4÷(2+3)	Ratio	0.90	1.32
B.	Conventional method 5÷2	Ratio	2.66	2.49
C.	Shepherds Method (ME) 1÷2	Ratio	5.04	5.76

The marketing efficiency according to Acharya's method (modified measure of marketing efficiency) under different marketing channels *i.e.* channel-I and channel-II was 0.90, 1.32 and 0.53, 1.05 in Delhi and Hisar/Bhiwani markets, respectively. According to Acharya's method, the marketing efficiency in channel-

III at Hisar/Bhiwani market was 1.42 and 3.41 in channel-IV at local/farm level market. Therefore, it can be appraised that channel IV is the most efficient among all marketing channels in the study area. This may because of the fact that the involvement of intermediaries is not apparent in channel-IV.

Table 4.16: Marketing Efficiency of Strawberry in Hisar/Bhiwani Markets under different Marketing Channels

Sl.No.	*Particulars*	*Unit*	*Channels*		
			I	*II*	*III*
1.	Consumer purchase price/retailer sale price (RP)	(₹/kg)	105.60	75.25	102.50
2.	Total marketing cost (MC)	(₹/kg)	22.70	15.65	15.65
3.	Total net margins of intermediaries (MM)	(₹/kg)	46.30	21.00	26.70
4.	Net price received by producers (FP)	(₹/kg)	36.60	38.60	60.15
5.	Value added (1-4)	(₹/kg)	69.00	36.65	42.35
	Index of marketing efficiency				
A	Acharya's method (MME) 4÷(2+3)	Ratio	0.53	1.05	1.42
B	Conventional method 5÷2	Ratio	3.04	2.34	2.71
C	Shepherds Method (ME) 1÷2	Ratio	4.65	4.81	6.55

The marketing efficiency according to conventional method under different marketing channel *i.e.* channel-I, channel-II were 2.66 and 2.49 in Delhi, 3.04 and 2.34 at Hisar/Bhiwani markets. The efficiency of channel-III and channel-IV through conventional method was 2.71 and 1.00 at Hisar/Bhiwani and local/farm level markets respectively. From this analysis, it could be observed that channel-I was the most efficient among all other marketing channels. Marketing efficiency of channel-I and channel-II through Shepherd's method were 5.04, 5.76 and 4.65, 4.81 in Delhi and Hisar/Bhiwani markets, respectively. The efficiency of channel-III and channel-IV through Shepherd's method was found to be 6.55 and 4.41. Therefore, according to Shepherd's method, channel-III is the most efficient among all other marketing channels.

Table 4.17: Marketing Efficiency of Strawberry in Local/Farm Level under Marketing Channel-IV

Sl.No.	*Particulars*	*Unit*	*Channel-IV*
1.	Retailer sale price (RP)	(₹/kg)	55.55
2.	Total marketing cost (MC)	(₹/kg)	12.60
3.	Total net margins of intermediaries (MM)	(₹/kg)	0.00
4.	Net price received by producers (FP)	(₹/kg)	42.95
5.	Value added (1-4)	(₹/kg)	12.60
	Index of marketing efficiency		
A	Acharya's method (MME) 4÷(2+3)	Ratio	3.41
B	Conventional method 5÷2	Ratio	1.00
C	Shepherds Method (ME) 1÷2	Ratio	4.41

4.3.6 Marketing Efficiency on the Basis of Producer's Share in Consumer's Rupee

The analysis of marketing efficiency of different channels in different markets shows that the marketing efficiency was found to be highest under the channel-IV and it was due to absence of marketing cost. The marketing efficiency ranked second for the channel-III in the market of Hisar and Bhiwani where the price spread has been estimated ₹ 42.35 per kg but slightly better price was offered for the produce (Table 4.18). The next efficient channel was observed to be the channel-II in the market of Delhi where the price spread was estimated to be ₹ 76.54 per kg and price offered of ₹ 100.96 per kg which was highest price. The fourth efficient channel was channel-II in the market of Hisar/Bhiwani in which price spread was ₹ 36.65 per kg. From the analysis one thing was very clear that the marketing margin comparative to marketing cost across the channels in different markets has been observed to be high and this need to check for improving further. Further, the channel-III in the market of Hisar and Bhiwani and channel-II in the market of Delhi need to strengthened to enhance its efficiency in better way. Although, the channel need to see according to their popularity among the farmers from produce disposal point of views. As the channel-II was found second largest disposal channel in Azadpur market Delhi and Hisar/Bhiwani markets.

Table 4.18: Marketing Efficiency of different Channels in Strawberry Marketing

Particulars	*Marketing Channels in different Selected Markets*					
	Delhi		*Hisar/Bhiwani*			*Local/Farm*
	I	*II*	*I*	*II*	*III*	*IV*
Average selling price (₹/q)	100.96 (47.23)	100.96 (56.88)	36.60 (34.66)	38.60 (51.30)	60.15 (58.68)	42.95 (77.32)
Marketing cost (₹/q)	42.37	30.79	22.70	15.65	15.65	12.60
Marketing margin (₹/q)	70.42	45.75	46.30	21.00	26.70	0.00
Price Spread	114.79	78.54	71.00	38.65	44.35	14.60
Marketing efficiency	0.90	1.32	0.53	1.05	1.42	3.41
Rank	**V**	**III**	**VI**	**IV**	**II**	**I**

Note: Figures in the parentheses are percentage of producer share in consumer's rupee.

Source: Field Survey (2015-16).

4.4 Problems Faced by Strawberry Grower and Traders

4.4.1 Problems Faced by Strawberry Grower

The problems faced by farming community regarding agricultural enterprises has attained a paramount significance since it acts as important source for the policy makers for formulation of policies for the welfare of farming community. The selected strawberry growers were contacted through opinion survey for analysing the problems in production as well as in the marketing of strawberry in the study area. They expressed number of problems, which are presented in Table 4.19. The detailed enquiry into these problems will help in exploring the opportunities for enhancing strawberry production and marketing efficiency in the study area. The problems were classified into production and marketing, among production problems 98.50 per cent of the grower stated that the runners propagation was not

Table 4.19: Problems Faced by Strawberry Grower

Particular	*Frequency*
A) Problems faced by strawberry grower during production	
Inability to reproduce the runners in this area	197 (98.50)
High value of initial investment	195 (97.50)
High cost of production due to unsuccessful sprouting of runner	193 (96.50)
High price of runners	190 (95.00)
Attack of pest and diseases	187 (93.50)
Non-availability of labour	183 (91.50)
Unfavourable climate condition	170 (85.00)
Poor quality of land	142 (71.00)
Non-availability of quality of runners	138 (69.00)
Lack of information on government subsidy	125 (62.50)
Unavailability of runners in time	115 (57.50)
Lack of water availability for irrigation	113 (56.50)
Lack of finance at reasonable rate of interest	108 (54.00)
No provision of technical support from state extension staff	80 (40.00)
Lack of knowledge of recommended practices	75 (37.50)
B) Problems faced by strawberry grower during Marketing	
Lack of storage facilities	200 (100.00)
Non-availability of agro processing unit	195 (97.50)
No provision of minimum support price	183 (91.50)
Low price due to seasonal glut	162 (81.00)
Highly perishable fruit	158 (79.00)
Delayed payment by the wholesaler/retailer	145 (72.50)
Lack of demand in local markets	133 (66.50)
Predominance of commission agent in the marketing system	125 (62.50)
High cost of packaging material	112 (56.00)
Non-availability of market	108 (54.00)
Lack of proper market information	87 (43.50)
Lack of transportation	83 (41.50)
Total	**200 (100.00)**

Note: Figures in the parentheses are percentage to the total.

possible on their fields due inability to reproduce the runners. About 97.50 per cent of growers were reported higher establishment cost at the initial stage of strawberry cultivation is the major financial constraints for resource poor farmers. 96.50 percent strawberry growers stated lower success rate of runners. High cost of runners was reported by 95 per cent of growers which limited their strawberry cultivation, as the runners not produced in Haryana State and it purchased from abroad or outside from the state *i.e.*, Himachal Pradesh. Disease and pest as production problems were faced by the ninety three percent strawberry growers. More than ninety percent respondents reported that labour scarcity is the major problem because strawberry is highly labour intensive crop. Eighty five percent of the strawberry growers were opined that very fragile and highly sensitivity of strawberry crop towards unfavourable climatic conditions such as hails storm and other unfavourable climate condition. More than 60 percent of the strawberry growers reported that non availability of proper technical knowhow from Department regarding strawberry cultivation. Timely availability of runners as well as quality water for irrigation purpose also was observed as the major production problem in the strawberry cultivation (56.50 per cent). Lower productivity of strawberry was also reported the production problem due to the sandy soil texture (71 per cent) and extreme hot as well as cold weather conditions in the study area (85 per cent).

As far as marketing problems of strawberry was concerned, 100 per cent of strawberry growers were reported lack of scientific storage facilities followed by non-availability of agro processing units (97.50 per cent), no provision of minimum support price (91.50 per cent), lower of prices due to seasonal glut (81 per cent), delay in payment by the wholesaler/retailer (72.50 per cent), lower demand in local markets (66.50 per cent), predominance of commission agent in the marketing system (62.50 per cent), high cost of packaging material (56 per cent), lack of transportation facilities (41.50 per cent) and lack of proper market information (43.50 per cent) in the study area.

Table 4.20: Problems Faced by Strawberry Retailers

Particular	*Frequency*
Lack of storage facilities	20 (100.00)
Wastage and spoilage	19 (95.00)
Highly perishable fruit	18 (92.50)
Lower demand by consumers in local markets	16 (82.50)
Non-availability of agro processing unit	10(52.50)
Total	**20 (100.00)**

Note: Figures in the parentheses are percentage to the total.

4.4.2 Problems Faced by Retailers

Strawberry marketing problems related to retailers in the study area are presented in Table 4.20, all the surveyed retailers respondents of strawberry were reported lack of scientific storage facilities followed by wastage and spoilage (95 per cent), highly perishable nature of strawberry fruit (92.50 per cent), Lower demand by consumers in local markets (82.50 per cent), non-availability of agro processing units (52.50 per cent) were observed as the major retailers related marketing problems in the study area.

4.4.3 Constraints Faced in Production and Marketing of Strawberry by the Growers

The constraints faced by the farmers in production of strawberry are shown in Table 4.21. According to results 15 constraints have been reported by the strawberry growers. The results reveals that majority of the farmers opined that inability to reproduce the runners hence, it ranks first with the highest Garrett score 76.40 followed by high value of initial investment, high cost of production due to unsuccessful sprouting of runner, high price of runners, attack of pest and diseases, non-availability of labour, Unfavourable climate condition *etc.* accounting second, third, fourth, fifth, sixth and seventh position with Garrett scores 73.37, 67.50, 61.81, 50.92, 52.23, 38.70, respectively (Table 4.21).

The problems faced in marketing of strawberry are presented in Table 4.22. According to results 12 constraints have been reported by the strawberry growers. Majority of the farmers opined that lack of storage facilities is the major problem in marketing hence, it ranks first with the highest Garrett score 81.34 followed by Non-availability of agro processing unit, highly perishable fruit, Low price due to seasonal glut, Non-provision of minimum support price, delayed payment by the wholesaler/retailer, lack of demand in local markets *etc.* accounting second, third, fourth, fifth and sixth position with Garrett score of 59.69, 55.50, 55.48, 46.39 and 38.39, respectively (Table 4.22).

4.4.4 Constraints Faced in Trading of Strawberry by the Traders

The problems faced in marketing of strawberry by the traders are presented in Table 4.23. According to results 5 constraints have been reported by the strawberry traders. Majority of the traders have opined that lack of storage facilities is the major problem in trading of strawberry hence, it ranks first with the highest Garrett score 63.60 followed by wastage and spoilage, highly perishable fruit, Low demand by consumers in local markets and non-availability of agro processing unit accounting second, third, fourth and fifth position with Garrett scores 48.40, 45.35, 36.40 and 21.95, respectively (Table 4.23).

It reveals from the above discussion that every strawberry grower has many problems in respect of sustainable cultivation practices and marketing of strawberry. Majority of respondents had faced constraint of inability to reproduce runners, high value of initial investment, high cost of production due to unsuccessful sprouting of runner, high price of runners, attack of pests and diseases, non-availability of labour *etc.* It is also highlighted that majority of the growers could not obtain remunerative prices for their product due to lack of information about market prices of different markets. It has been also found that since the initial investment is very high in strawberry cultivation, the subsidies on drip irrigation system may be increased. Availability of bio-insecticide and bio-pesticides at cheaper rate and the practical

Table 4.21: Garrett Ranking for Constraints in Production of Strawberry by the Growers

Sl. No.	Problems	Rank given by the Growers																	
		1st	2nd	3rd	4th	5th	6th	7th	8th	9th	10th	11th	12th	13th	14th	15th	Total	per cent	Rank
1.	Inability to reproduce the runners in this area	8364	4800	1725	390	0	0	0	0	0	0	0	0	0	0	0	**15279**	**76.40**	**I**
2.	High value of initial investment	4838	6450	2415	910	61	0	0	0	0	0	0	0	0	0	0	**14674**	**73.37**	**II**
3.	High cost of production due to unsuccessful sprouting of runner	1968	1875	6762	1495	1342	57	0	0	0	0	0	0	0	0	0	**13499**	**67.50**	**III**
4.	High price of runners	574	525	1380	6955	2135	684	108	0	0	0	0	0	0	0	0	**12361**	**61.81**	**IV**
5.	Attack of pests and diseases	164	0	0	520	3782	2679	1404	150	188	176	520	396	155	50	0	**10184**	**50.92**	**VI**
6.	Non-availability of labour	820	900	1587	2275	488	342	270	700	987	1452	480	144	0	0	0	**10445**	**52.23**	**V**
7.	Unfavourable climate condition	164	0	0	0	305	1197	972	1200	705	616	1000	1116	465	0	0	**7740**	**38.70**	**VII**
8.	Poor quality of land	0	0	0	0	0	285	216	450	752	1452	1400	864	341	125	0	**5885**	**29.43**	**XII**
9.	Non-availability of quality of runners	0	0	0	0	1891	2280	1944	1050	423	44	0	0	0	0	0	**7632**	**38.16**	**VIII**

Sl. No.	Problems	Rank given by the Growers															Total	per cent	Rank
		1st	2nd	3rd	4th	5th	6th	7th	8th	9th	10th	11th	12th	13th	14th	15th			
10.	Lack of information on government subsidy	0	0	0	0	732	798	756	1100	705	1100	640	252	0	0	0	**6083**	**30.42**	**IX**
11.	Unavailability of runners in time	0	0	0	0	244	1254	1944	1750	799	44	0	0	0	0	0	**6035**	**30.18**	**X**
12.	Lack of water availability for irrigation	0	0	0	0	549	1083	1782	1400	987	88	40	0	0	0	0	**5929**	**29.65**	**XI**
13.	Lack of finance at reasonable rate of interest	0	0	0	0	549	627	1134	1150	1551	440	40	0	0	0	0	**5491**	**27.46**	**XIII**
14.	No provision of technical support from state extension staff	0	0	0	0	122	171	378	300	1222	968	280	180	62	0	0	**3683**	**18.42**	**XIV**
15.	Lack of knowledge of recommended practices	0	0	0	0	122	0	108	350	799	1012	640	252	31	0	0	**3314**	**16.57**	XV

Table 4.22: Garrett Ranking for Constraints in Marketing of Strawberry by the Growers

Sl. No.	Problems	Rank given by the Growers														
		1st	2nd	3rd	4th	5th	6th	7th	8th	9th	10th	11th	12th	Total	per cent	Rank
1.	Lack of storage facilities	13440	2627	201	0	0	0	0	0	0	0	0	0	16268	81.34	**I**
2.	Non-availability of agro processing unit	0	1775	2680	4026	2337	636	144	220	120	0	0	0	11938	59.69	**II**
3.	Highly perishable fruit	1848	5680	2278	671	570	53	0	0	0	0	0	0	11100	55.50	**III**
4.	Low price due to seasonal glut	1428	3692	3283	915	912	530	48	88	0	0	0	0	10896	54.48	**IV**
5.	Non-provision of minimum support price	0	71	536	915	1539	2226	1824	1276	720	170	0	0	9277	46.39	**V**
6.	Delayed payment by the wholesaler/ retailer	0	71	402	671	1824	2226	1968	396	120	0	0	0	7678	38.39	**VI**
7.	Lack of demand in local markets	84	71	871	1708	1026	1590	1056	440	400	0	0	0	7246	36.23	**VII**
9.	High cost of packaging material	84	0	1072	1830	1710	1113	528	132	0	0	0	0	6469	32.35	**VIII**
10.	Predominance of commission agent in the marketing system	0	0	67	305	798	1484	1728	1452	280	34	0	0	6148	30.74	**IX**
11.	Non-availability of market	0	0	67	183	228	159	960	2156	960	136	0	0	4849	24.25	**X**
12.	Lack of transportation	0	0	1742	610	513	318	240	484	600	34	0	0	4541	22.71	**XI**
13.	Lack of proper market information	0	0	0	0	0	265	912	1100	1240	204	28	0	3749	18.75	XII

knowledge regarding plant protection and fertilizer application at proper tim should be imparted to the growers.

Table 4.23: Garrett Ranking for Constraints in Trading of Strawberry by the Traders

Sl. No.	Problems	Rank given by the Traders							
		1st	2nd	3rd	4th	5th	Total	per cent	Rank
1.	Lack of storage facilities	760	122	350	40	0	1272	63.60	I
2.	Wastage and spoilage	152	366	200	200	50	968	48.40	II
3.	Highly perishable fruit	228	244	200	160	75	907	45.35	III
4.	Low demand by consumers in local markets	152	61	200	240	75	728	36.40	IV
5.	Non-availability of agro processing unit	152	122	0	40	125	439	21.95	V

Chapter 5

Summary and Conclusions

The state of Haryana has ample scope of production of fruits, vegetables, and flowers, spices mushroom, medicinal and aromatic plants. The cultivation of horticulture crops is highly specialized, technical and remunerative venture as compared to traditional crops being grown by the farmers. Apart from this, majority of Horticulture crops, being perishable in nature, requires systematic planning for their development. Horticulture development has assumed greater importance in recent years since this sector has been identified as remunerative for diversification of land use which provides increased employment opportunities, better return per unit area besides filling the nutritional gaps. Farmers in Haryana have also started taking up horticulture crops as a separate viable economic activity, with a view to give a boost to the growth of horticulture in the state. Haryana is one of the 29 states in India, situated in North India. It was carved out of the former state of East Punjab on 1 November 1966 on a linguistic basis. It stands 21st in terms of its area, which is spread about 44,212 km^2. It has tremendously developed itself in terms of economy and progressing in production of fruits and vegetables. It is known as an agrarian state, as most of the people depend on agriculture. The state having rich source of horticulture crops such as fruits, vegetables *etc.* The agro climatic condition of Haryana is suitable for growing of many kinds of fruits *viz.*, Grapes, Kinnow, Malta, Mango, Ber, Guava, Peach, and Papaya. Suitable varieties are popular among farmers. There is a great scope of increase the area under Horticulture crops.

The area under fruit crops during 2015-16 in Haryana has been recorded as 60.92 ha with a production of 737.82 MT (GoH, 2016). Among the fruits, strawberry is one of the most important fruit grown in Haryana which gives an immense income to the livelihood of the farmer. It is known as a low volume high value crop and grows well under protected and open condition. It can be easily grown in state of Haryana. It gives quickest return in short time than any other fruit crops. The total area under strawberry in the state during 2015-16 was 140 ha with a total production of 1651 MT (GoH, 2016). Strawberry from the state is being sold in Delhi market. It is also exported to Bhutan, Nepal, Bangladesh and various other countries.

Haryana, one of the 29 states of country which has an immense scope for strawberry production as the climatic condition is highly favourable for the crop. The growers also can receive comparatively higher profit on selling the fruit due to its high value in nature. Hence, producing strawberry is becoming an alternative source of income for the farmers of the state. But unfortunately, despite of strawberry being profitable, it could spread and it might be due to unaware about the profitability of the crop. They are also not well aware about the proper marketing channel and marketing strategy to be followed for getting the due share of producers in consumer's rupee. Shortage of runners (seedling) which are not readily available in their farm has become a matter of concern in the recent past. On the contrary organised market for strawberry made the traders/middlemen the major players in marketing of strawberry. Keeping all these into consideration, the present study on strawberry cultivation is an imperative as there is no such type of study carried out in this regard.

Hence, keeping in view the importance of the crop and the various problematic situations associated with strawberry cultivation, the present research study entitled "Study on Production and Marketing of Strawberry in Haryana, India" has been undertaken with the following specific objectives.

5.1 Objectives

The specific objectives of the study are:

1. To work out the economics of strawberry in Haryana state;
2. To study the marketing practices and channels involved in marketing of strawberry in the state;
3. To estimate the marketing costs, margins and price spread for the strawberry; and
4. To identify the problems faced by the producers and traders in the production and marketing of strawberry.

5.2 Database and Methodology

The study has been conducted based upon the survey method. In this method, the investigator sampled a group of individuals, and their responses to the questions were asked and recorded. This was done through personal interviewing method. The investigator used pre-structured scheduled to collect the relevant information from the individuals. Haryana is divided into four divisions for administrative purposes; they are Ambala, Gurgram, Hisar and Rohtak. Within these divisions there are 22 districts, 47 sub-divisions, 67 tehsils, 45 sub-tehsils and 116 blocks. There are total 81 cities and towns in Haryana and 6,759 villages. As per the latest available secondary information, the area and production of strawberry are highest in Hisar and Bhiwani districts of Haryana. Thus, Hisar and Bhiwani districts of Haryana were selected purposively for the present study.

Hisar district comprises of nine blocks. Out of these nine blocks, Hisar-1 block was selected purposively based on the highest area and production of strawberry. Bhiwani district comprises of seven blocks. Similarly out of these seven blocks, Siwani block was selected purposively based on the highest area and production of strawberry.

A list of all villages of selected blocks of both the selected district was prepared with the area under strawberry of individual farmer. Finally, two villages namely Sahadawa, SatrodKhurd from Hisar-1 block of Hisar district and Chanana and Siwani villages from Siwani block of Bhiwani district were selected randomly for the present study.

A comprehensive list of total strawberry growers of the four selected villages has been prepared and then it has been categorised into three categories based on their land holdings *viz.*, small (up to 2.0 ha.), medium (2.10 to 4.00) and large (>4.00 ha.). It has been found that there are 316 strawberry growers in these four villages. Finally, 200 strawberry growers were selected by employing the probability proportional to size as the ultimate sample unit of the study.

It has been found that Azadpur market is the major market for strawberry both for Hisar and Bhiwani districts because more than 80 per cent of the produce of these districts is merchandised through this market. Thus Azadpur market was selected purposively to study the different market functionaries associated with marketing of strawberry. While collecting the primary information, it has been found that four major channels are connected towards marketing of strawberry. The major identified channels are studied in depth in order to conducting a comprehensive study on marketing and marketing functionaries of strawberry in the study area. Suitable economic and statistical tools have been employed for precise and better analysis and interpretation of the data.

5.3 Main Findings

The initial cost (establishment cost) of cultivation consists of land drip irrigation, permanent fencing, and low tunnel. Total cost of establishment of strawberry orchard per ha was observed to be highest in small category of orchard which was followed by medium and large category with the amount of ₹ 153.93 thousand, ₹ 145.18 thousand and ₹ 144.08 thousand per ha, respectively. Overall, it was estimated ₹ 149.55 thousand per ha across the categories. The cost incurred for strawberry required adequate water for its better growth and production, therefore irrigation facilities was required to meet the water requirement for the crop hence, the cost incurred on drip irrigation was estimated to be 46.82 per cent of total cost in small category, followed by medium (42.99 per cent) and large (38.40 per cent) category of farms.

The fencing is also required for protection of strawberry orchard from Nilgai (Blue Bull) and Chital like wild animals which are exists in large numbers in the study area. The cost incurred for fencing was estimated highest on large farms and followed by medium and small category of farms and it contributed 27.16 per cent, 25.87 per cent and 23.91 per cent of the total establishment cost respectively. In this part of the country, generally temperature remains more than 30°C during the month of September to October *i.e.* sowing time of strawberry, and remains lower less than 3° C during the month of December and January, both the extreme weather condition leads to serious damage to the crop, therefore, farmers' use plastic sheets as low tunnel to protect their crop from abrupt weather conditions. However, the costs incurred for low tunnel for various categories have been contributed 34.44 per cent on large farms, followed by medium (31.84 per cent) and small (29.27 per cent) category of farms. Similarly, per hectare overall establishment cost across the different farm categories was estimated 43.99 per cent on drip irrigation, 30.95 per cent on low tunnel and 25.06 per cent contributed as cost of permanent fencing.

Strawberry is a seasonal crop and required cost to perform petty operations time to time. The total operational cost in case of small category of farms was accounted to be ₹ 670.35 thousand per ha in which the major cost incurred on runners and it accounted to be 47.65 per cent of the total cost. Second major cost was observed plant protection *i.e.* 13.16 per cent followed by cost incurred on hired human (10.84 per cent), costs of manure (5.01 per cent), replacement cost (4.69 per cent), irrigation (3.78 per cent), fertilizers costs (3.62 per cent), picking (2.39 per cent), preparation of land (0.95 per cent), and bed preparation (0.28 per cent).

On medium category of farms, the total operational cost was worked out to be ₹ 739.76 thousand per ha in which the major share contributed by cost of runners (43.89 per cent), followed by hired human labour (18.22 per cent), plant protection (11.60 per cent), replacement cost (4.28 per cent), manure (4.23 per cent), fertilizers costs (3.52 per cent), irrigation (3.48 per cent) picking (2.12 per cent), preparation of land (0.77 per cent), and bed preparation (0.24 per cent). Similarly, the total operation cost in case of large category of farms was estimated to be ₹ 791.43 thousand per ha. Among the total operational cost the major cost was found on runners (41.39 per cent) followed by hired human labour (24.64 per cent), plant protection (9.67 per cent), replacement cost (4.16 per cent), fertilizers costs (3.74 per cent), manure (3.03 per cent), irrigation (2.98 per cent), picking (1.89 per cent), preparation of land (0.63 per cent), and bed preparation (0.21 per cent).Overall, the total operational cost, across the different categories of farms was estimated to be ₹ 713.64 thousand per ha revealed that the overall highest operational cost accounted to be 45.19 per cent on runners followed by hired human labour (16.01 per cent), plant protection (11.94 per cent), replacement cost (4.46 per cent),manure (4.35 per cent),fertilizers costs (3.62 per cent),irrigation (3.52 per cent), picking (2.20 per cent), preparation of land (0.83 per cent) and bed preparation (0.26 per cent) in the study area.

The marketing cost is maximum in case of small category of farms which was accounted to be ₹ 294.86 thousand per ha followed by medium *i.e.* ₹ 279.10 and large category of farms *i.e.* ₹ 264.38 per ha in which the major cost incurred on packing material and it accounted for 65.29, 64.36 and 63.31 per cent of total marketing cost on small, medium and large category of farms. Second major cost component was transportation cost. It was observed highest on large category of farms *i.e.* 28.70 per cent followed by medium (28.12 per cent) and small category of farms (27.56 per cent).Other marketing cost was packing cost incurred 6.11, 5.58, and 5.17 per cent of large, medium and small category of farms, respectively, whereas unloading charges was accounted 1.99 per cent on small, 1.94 per cent on medium and 1.88 per cent on large category of farms. Overall, the total marketing cost, across the different categories of farms was estimated to be ₹ 284.44 thousand per ha in which highest marketing cost accounted to be 64.66 per cent on packing materials, followed by transportation (27.92 per cent), packing cost (5.46 per cent) and unloading charges (1.96 per cent) in the study area.

The total costs of strawberry cultivation including family labour per ha have been worked out to be ₹ 905.04 thousand, ₹ 947.65 thousand, ₹ 970.10 thousand on small, medium, large category of strawberry growers, respectively in which more than 91 per cent share contributed by variable cost on small, medium and 92 per cent share on large category of strawberry growers. The total cost found to be higher on large category of farms mainly due to more use of hired labour, runners, plastic mulching and fertilizers measures comparative to medium and small category of strawberry growers. Similarly, the cost of runners, hired labour, family labour and plant protection were found to be higher cost components in overall cost which shared 34.66 per cent, 12.28 per cent, 12.17 per cent and 9.16 per cent of overall total cost of strawberry cultivation *i.e.* ₹ 930.39 thousand per ha.

It reveals from the analysis that Cost A worked out to be ₹ 719.45 thousand, ₹ 792.19 thousand and ₹ 844.49 thousand per ha on small, medium and large categories of strawberry growers. The cost incurred on purchasing of runners, marketing cost and hired labour was the major components of Cost A on all categories of the strawberry growers in the study area. The overall Cost A was worked out to be ₹ 764.39 thousand per ha across the different categories of farms, in which 34.12 per cent of runners cost observed as the major cost component followed by hired labour (12.08 per cent) and plant protection (9.01 per cent). The Cost B on small, medium, large category of strawberry farms worked to be ₹ 785.30 thousand, ₹ 861.02 thousand and ₹ 912.34 thousand per ha, respectively.

The overall cost of strawberry cultivation was worked out to be ₹ 832.04 thousand per ha across the different categories of strawberry growers. The Cost C have been worked out to be ₹ 989.23 thousand per ha on large category of strawberry growers which was observed as highest followed by medium (₹ 963.87 thousand per ha) and small (₹ 917.85 thousand per ha) category of strawberry growers. The overall cost of strawberry cultivation was estimated to be ₹ 945.29 thousand per ha across the different categories of strawberry growers. Hence, all these costs *i.e.* Cost A, Cost B and Cost C were found to be increased with the increase of size of the strawberry orchard in the study area.

The yield of strawberry cultivation was estimated to be highest in case of small (16007.82 kg/ha) category of strawberry growers followed by medium (15678.20 kg/ha) and large (14992.74 kg/ha) farms, whereas, the overall yield was worked out to be 15714.16 kg/ha in the study area. The gross farm income was worked out to be ₹ 2109.03 thousand, ₹ 2120.48 thousand and ₹ 2101.98 thousand on small, medium and large categories of strawberry growers, respectively. The overall gross income of strawberry growers was estimated to be ₹ 2111.98 thousand per ha. Whereas net return including the family labour was worked out to be higher on small (₹ 1191.18 thousand/ha) followed by medium (₹ 1156.61 thousand/ha) and large (₹ 1112.75 thousand/ha) categories of strawberry growers. Similarly, the net return excluding the family labour was worked out to be highest on small, followed by medium and large categories of strawberry growers which was accounted to be ₹ 1323.73 thousand, ₹ 1259.46 thousand and ₹ 1189.64 thousand per ha, respectively. The farm business income of small, medium and large categories of strawberry growers was worked out to be ₹ 1389.58 thousand, ₹ 1328.29 thousand and ₹ 1257.49 thousand per ha in the study area. The overall farm business income was estimated to be ₹ 1347.59 thousand per ha across the various categories of strawberry growers. The family labour income was worked out to be higher on small category of strawberry growers *i.e.* ₹ 1323.73 thousand per ha. followed by medium (₹ 1259.46 thousand/ha.) and large (₹ 1189.64 thousand/ha.) categories of strawberry growers.

The overall family labour income was worked out to be ₹ 1279.94 thousand per ha across the different categories of strawberry growers. The farm investment income of strawberry growers was estimated to be highest on small category (₹ 1191.18 thousand/ha) followed by medium (₹ 1156.61 thousand/ha) and large (₹ 1112.75 thousand/ha) categories of strawberry growers. Overall the farm investment income from strawberry worked out to be ₹ 1166.69 thousand per ha across the different categories of farms. The Benefit Cost Ratio (BCR) over paid out cost A of strawberry cultivation over total cost was worked out to be higher on small category of strawberry growers (2.93) followed by medium (2.68) and large (2.49) categories of farms whereas the Benefit Cost Ratio over paid out cost B was worked out to be 2.69, 2.46 and 2.30 on small, medium and large categories of strawberry growers, respectively.

Similarly, the Benefit Cost Ratio over paid out cost C was worked out to be higher on small category of strawberry growers (2.30) followed by medium (2.20) and large (2.12) categories of farms. All these facts indicate that strawberry cultivation is profitable in the study area.

Effort has been made in this to use the non-parametric DEA analysis to obtain the technical efficiency scores (under variable returns to scale) in measuring efficiency of the individual firms. We define efficiency as a measure of how efficiently the inputs are employed to achieve a given level of output. Inefficiency occurs owing to lack of managerial oversight of the production process. A farm is considered to be inefficient if it could produce the same output using fewer inputs (input oriented) or it could produce more output using same input (output oriented). It is worthwhile to note that in this DEA analysis, as individual farms may not be operating at their optimum scale, we consider *Variable Returns to Scale (VRS)* in our *Output-Oriented* DEA model. Hence, the efficiency scores thus obtained essentially indicate *Pure Technical Efficiency (PTE)* of individual farms.

It is easy to find here that this *multi-input multi output* DEA analysis shows that the pure technical efficiency of the strawberry farms increase steadily with low holding size, which calls for newer wave of modernization drive in the higher size class in Haryana. In this multi-input multi-output model, the outputs are total production of strawberry. The inputs are fixed costs, variable costs, market incidentals (including depreciation) incurred by the firms.

The marketable and marketed surplus of strawberry was found to be equal for all categories of farm. The requirement of strawberry for family consumption for different purposes was observed comparatively high on large (0.055 per cent) category of farms, followed by medium (0.039 per cent) and small (0.025 per cent) category of farms, whereas at overall level it was found to be 0.035 per cent of total produce. The retention capacity was observed more on large category of farms may be due to large size of family as compared to medium and small farms. The quantity retained in household across the different categories of farms was found to be 5.43 kg which was shared by quantity used for spoilage (0.015 per cent), as major share followed by family consumption (0.009 per cent), social obligation (0.006 per cent) and religious purpose (0.004 per cent). Hence, from the above discussion, it may be concluded that strawberry has its importance in spiritual/religious sphere too. The marketable and marketed surplus found to be equal because of its perishability.

Four major marketing channels were identified for disposal off strawberry from the producers to the ultimate consumer. Comparing the results for different channels, it was observed that producer's share in consumer's rupee was highest in direct sale in comparison to the channels where there are different intermediaries. In channels- I and II, net prices received by the producers was found to be 47.23 per cent and 56.88 per cent in Azadpur market (Delhi) and 34.66 per cent and 51.31 per cent of consumer's price in Hisar/Bhiwani market, respectively. Whereas in channels- III and IV the net price received by producer was per cent and 58.68 per cent and 77.32 per cent of consumer's price in Hisar/Bhiwani and Local market, respectively. This clearly shows that producer's share in consumer's rupee decreases with the increase in the number of intermediaries. However, the point should be noted here that volume of transaction is high through channels- I and II in Hisar/Bhiwani market even the producer's share in consumer's rupee is high in channel-IV. This occurs because local market is unable to consume the total volume of production due to lack of local demand at the initial stage of production.

There are some simple measures to assess the efficiency of the marketing system for agricultural commodities (Acharya *et al.*, 1987). The analysis of marketing efficiency of different channels in different markets shows that the marketing efficiency was found to be highest in channel-IV and it was due to absence of marketing cost. The marketing efficiency ranked second for the channel-III in the market of Hisar and Bhiwani where the price spread has been estimated ₹ 42.35 per kg but slightly better price was offered for the produce. The next efficient channel was observed to be the channel-II in the market of Delhi where the price spread was estimated to be ₹ 76.54 per kg and price offered of ₹ 100.96 per kg which was highest price. The fourth efficient channel was channel-II in the market of Hisar/Bhiwani in which price spread was ₹ 36.65 per kg. From the analysis one thing was very clear that the marketing margin comparative to marketing cost across the channels in different markets has been observed to be high and this need to check for improving further. Further, the channel-III in the market of Hisar and Bhiwani and channel-II in the market of Delhi need to strengthened to enhance its efficiency in better way. The channel needs to see according to their popularity among the farmers from produce disposal point of views as the channel-II was found second largest disposal channel in Azadpur market Delhi and Hisar/Bhiwani markets.

The problems faced by farming community regarding agricultural enterprises has attained a paramount significance since it acts as important source for the policy makers for formulation of policies for the welfare of farming community. The problems were classified into production and marketing, among production problems 98.50 per cent of the grower stated that the runners propagation was not possible on their fields due inability to reproduce the runners. About 97.50 per cent of growers were reported higher establishment cost at the initial stage of strawberry cultivation is the major financial constraints for resource poor farmers. 96.50 percent strawberry growers stated lower success rate of runners. High cost of runners was reported by 95 per cent of growers which limited their strawberry cultivation, as the runners not produced in Haryana State and it purchased from abroad or outside from the state *i.e.* Himachal Pradesh. Disease and pest as production problems were faced by the ninety three percent strawberry growers. More than ninety percent respondents reported that labour scarcity is the major problem because strawberry is highly labour intensive crop. Eighty five percent of the strawberry growers were opined that very fragile and highly sensitivity of strawberry crop towards unfavourable climatic conditions such as hails storm and other unfavourable climate condition. More than 60 percent of the strawberry growers reported that non availability of proper technical knowhow from Department regarding strawberry cultivation. Timely availability of runners as well as quality water for irrigation purpose also was observed as the major production problem in the strawberry cultivation (56.50 per cent). Lower productivity of strawberry was also reported the production problem due to the sandy soil texture (71 per cent) and extreme hot as well as cold weather conditions in the study area (85 per cent).

As far as marketing problems of strawberry was concerned, 100 per cent of strawberry growers were reported lack of scientific storage facilities followed by non-availability of agro processing units (97.50 per cent), no provision of minimum support price (91.50 per cent), lower of prices due to seasonal glut (81 per cent), delay in payment by the wholesaler/retailer (72.50 per cent), lower demand in local markets (66.50 per cent), predominance of commission agent in the marketing system (62.50 per cent), high cost of packaging material (56 per cent), lack of transportation facilities (41.50 per cent) and lack of proper market information (43.50 per cent) in the study area.

All the surveyed retailers respondents of strawberry were reported lack of scientific storage facilities followed by wastage and spoilage (95 per cent), highly perishable nature of strawberry fruit (92.50 per cent), Lower demand by consumers in local markets (82.50 per cent), non-availability of agro processing units (52.50 per cent) were observed as the major retailers related marketing problems in the study area. The information on various problems faced by producers and traders of strawberry in the study area were recorded from the respondents. Tabular analysis has been employed to examine the problems in cultivation and marketing of strawberry at the grass root levels.

Garrett's ranking technique was also used to evaluate the constraints faced by both growers and traders of strawberry. According to results 15 constraints have been reported by the strawberry growers. The results reveals that majority of the farmers opined that inability to reproduce the runners hence, it ranks first with the highest Garrett score 76.40 followed by high value of initial investment, high cost of production due to unsuccessful sprouting of runner, high price of runners, attack of pest and diseases, non-availability of labour, Unfavourable climate condition *etc.* accounting second, third, fourth, fifth, sixth and seventh position with Garrett scores 73.37, 67.50, 61.81, 50.92, 52.23, 38.70, respectively.

12 constraints have been reported by the growers in case of marketing of strawberry. Majority of the farmers opined that lack of storage facilities is the major problem in marketing hence, it ranks first with the highest Garrett score 81.34 followed by Non-availability of agro processing unit, highly perishable fruit, Low price due to seasonal glut, Non-provision of minimum support price, delayed payment by the wholesaler/retailer, lack of demand in local markets *etc.* accounting second, third, fourth, fifth and sixth position with Garrett score of 59.69, 55.50, 55.48, 46.39 and 38.39, respectively.

It has been found that 5 constraints have also been reported by the strawberry traders. Majority of the traders have opined that lack of storage facilities is the major problem in trading of strawberry hence, it ranks first with the highest Garrett score 63.60 followed by wastage and spoilage, highly perishable fruit, Low demand by consumers in local markets and non-availability of agro processing unit accounting second, third, fourth and fifth position with Garrett scores 48.40, 45.35, 36.40 and 21.95, respectively.

It reveals from the above discussion that every strawberry grower has many problems in respect of sustainable cultivation practices and marketing of strawberry. Majority of respondents had faced constraint of inability to reproduce runners, high value of initial investment, high cost of production due to unsuccessful sprouting of runner, high price of runners, attack of pests and diseases, non-availability of labour *etc.* It is also highlighted that majority of the growers could not obtain remunerative prices for their product due to lack of information about market prices of different markets. It has been also found that since the initial investment is very high in strawberry cultivation, the subsidies on drip irrigation system may be increased. Availability of bio-insecticide and bio-pesticides at cheaper rate and the practical knowledge regarding plant protection and fertilizer application at proper time should be imparted to the growers.

5.4 Conclusion

The present investigation was intended to depict the picture of the strawberry growing enterprise in Hisar and Bhiwani, the prominent strawberry growing districts in Haryana. The enterprise has assumed a pride of place in the economy of the tract as it is an important horticultural crop of the tract. In this investigation, it was found that strawberry is a profitable crop.

The overall cost of strawberry cultivation was worked out to be ₹ 832.04 thousand per ha across the different categories of strawberry growers. The Cost C have been worked out to be ₹ 989.23 thousand per ha on large category of strawberry growers which was observed as highest followed by medium (₹ 963.87 thousand per ha) and small (₹ 917.85 thousand per ha) category of strawberry growers. The overall cost of strawberry cultivation was estimated to be ₹ 945.29 thousand per ha across the different categories of strawberry growers. Hence, all these costs *i.e.* Cost A, Cost B and Cost C were found to be increased with the increase of size of the strawberry orchard in the study area.

The yield of strawberry cultivation was estimated to be highest in case of small (16007.82 kg/ha) category of strawberry growers followed by medium (15678.20 kg/ha) and large (14992.74 kg/ha) farms, whereas, the overall yield was worked out to be 15714.16 kg/ha in the study area. The gross farm income was worked out to be ₹ 2109.03 thousand, ₹ 2120.48 thousand and ₹ 2101.98 thousand on small, medium and large categories of strawberry growers, respectively. The overall gross income of strawberry growers was estimated to be ₹ 2111.98 thousand per ha. Whereas net return including the family labour was worked out to be higher on small (₹ 1191.18 thousand/ha) followed by medium (₹ 1156.61 thousand/ha) and large (₹ 1112.75 thousand/ha) categories of strawberry growers. Similarly, the net return excluding the family labour was worked out to be highest on small, followed by medium and large categories of strawberry growers which was accounted to be ₹ 1323.73 thousand, ₹ 1259.46 thousand and ₹ 1189.64 thousand per ha, respectively. The farm business income of small, medium and large categories of strawberry growers was worked out to be ₹ 1389.58 thousand, ₹ 1328.29 thousand and ₹ 1257.49 thousand per ha in the study area. The overall farm business income was estimated to be ₹ 1347.59 thousand per ha across the various categories of strawberry growers. The family labour income was worked out to be higher on small category of strawberry growers *i.e.* ₹ 1323.73 thousand per ha. followed by medium (₹ 1259.46 thousand/ha.) and large (₹ 1189.64 thousand/ha.) categories of strawberry growers.

The overall family labour income was worked out to be ₹ 1279.94 thousand per ha across the different categories of strawberry growers. The farm investment income of strawberry growers was estimated to be highest on small category (₹ 1191.18 thousand/ha) followed by medium (₹ 1156.61 thousand/ha) and large (₹ 1112.75 thousand/ha) categories of strawberry growers. Overall the farm investment income from strawberry worked out to be ₹ 1166.69 thousand per ha across the different categories of farms. The Benefit Cost Ratio (BCR) over paid out cost A of strawberry cultivation over total cost was worked out to be higher on small category of strawberry growers (2.93) followed by medium (2.68) and large (2.49) categories of farms whereas the Benefit Cost Ratio over paid out cost B was worked out to be 2.69, 2.46 and 2.30 on small, medium and large categories of strawberry growers, respectively.

Similarly, the Benefit Cost Ratio over paid out cost C was worked out to be higher on small category of strawberry growers (2.30) followed by medium (2.20) and large (2.12) categories of farms. All these facts indicate that strawberry cultivation is profitable in the study area.

The marketable and marketed surplus of strawberry was found to be equal or all categories of farm. The requirement of strawberry for family consumption or different purposes was observed comparatively high on large (0.055 per cent) ategory of farms, followed by medium (0.039 per cent) and small (0.025 per cent) ategory of farms, whereas at overall level it was found to be 0.035 per cent of total roduce. The retention capacity was observed more on large category of farms may e due to large size of family as compared to medium and small farms. The quantity etained in household across the different categories of farms was found to be 5.43 g which was shared by quantity used for spoilage (0.015 per cent), as major share ollowed by family consumption (0.009 per cent), social obligation (0.006 per cent) nd religious purpose (0.004 per cent). Hence, from the above discussion, it may e concluded that strawberry has its importance in spiritual/religious sphere too. The marketable and marketed surplus found to be equal because of its perishability.

It reveals from the results that every strawberry grower has many problems in espect of sustainable cultivation practices and marketing of strawberry. Majority of respondents had faced constraint of inability to reproduce runners, high value of nitial investment, high cost of production due to unsuccessful sprouting of runner, igh price of runners, attack of pests and diseases, non-availability of labour *etc.* t is also highlighted that majority of the growers could not obtain remunerative prices for their product due to lack of information about market prices of different markets. It has been also found that since the initial investment is very high in strawberry cultivation, the subsidies on drip irrigation system may be increased. Availability of bio-insecticide and bio-pesticides at cheaper rate and the practical knowledge regarding plant protection and fertilizer applications at proper time should be imparted to the growers.

Chapter 6

Way Forward

There are two main groups of commercial strawberries grown today, each with many cultivars. 'June - bearing or short - day' strawberries develop their flower buds in the shorter days of late summer and early fall, overwintering until the following spring when they produce fruit around June. Strawberry has advantages of easy propagation, early maturity and high yield with 5-9 per cent sugar. To boost its production there is a need to develop infra-structure facilities for transport of produce to primary markets as the fruit is highly perishable. Processing facilities in the major producing states have to be made for value addition. Therefore, there is a scope for future research in post-harvest management.

The strawberry growers are progressive farmers and they are always in touch with latest techniques of cultivation. Therefore, whatever, is within their reach, they try to do their best to obtain the good yields. Even then, all the strawberry growers cannot adopt good agronomic practice which are required to be carried out at proper time with due skill. Therefore, there is a scope to find out the gap between recommended and adopted practices by the growers at the field level. Government and Co-operative Associations should have combined efforts to tackle the constraints faced by the strawberry growers in respect of cultivation and marketing as well.

The points required to be considered by the institutional agencies are provision of adequate credit in time, provision of fertilizers, pesticides, fungicides and packing material at subsidised rates, provision of the high tech irrigation methods such as drip irrigation systems with good qualities at low rates by increasing the existing subsidy and there is also scope to conduct future research on strawberry and provide expert guidance service to strawberry growers relating not only with techniques of cultivation but also marketing aspects of strawberry. The necessary infrastructural facilities such as pre-cooling unit, cold storage facility, and refrigerated containers should make available.

As the research area of the present investigation was limited to some specific objectives, there is further scope to examine the significant factors associated with production and marketing of strawberry. It may be noted that provision of good infrastructure is essential for the development of agriculture/horticulture. So investments on infrastructure are of utmost importance. So the strawberry growers should be provided with physical infrastructures and support system and some basic infrastructures with the objective of promoting higher income.

References

Acharya, S.S. and Agarwal, N.L. (2011). Agricultural marketing in India.

Afridi, G.S.; Ishaq, M., and Ahmad, S. (2009). Cost and revenue analysis of strawberry production in the sub-tropical areas of NWFP, Pakistan. *Pak. j. life soc. sci.*, **7**(1): 59-65.

Ambad, S.N.; Patil, K.B.; Nevkar, G.S. and Kadam, V.S. (1995). Strawberry lagwadiche sudharit tantra. Shetkari, Sepetamber. **31**(5): 17-20.

Anchal, D. and Sharma, V.K. (2009). Price spread of Litchi in Punjab. *Indian Journal of Agricultural Marketing*, **23**(2): 147-153.

Anonymous (2009). Agro-Economic Research Centre (A.E.R.C) For North East India, Assam Agricultural University Jorhat, Assam. Potentialities of Horticultural Crops and Market Accessibilities in Assam and Meghalaya with Special Reference to Technology Mission for Integrated Development of Horticulture. *Agricultural Situation in India.* May. pp: 97-103.

Bachhal, G.S. (2016). Problems and prospect of strawberry cultivation in Haryana. Unpublished M.Sc. thesis, CCSHAU, Hisar.

Baite J. David. (2011). A Study on adoption of pineapple cultivation practices by the tribal farmers of Churachanpur District of Manipur. *M.Sc Thesis submitted to Central Agriculture University, Imphal.*

Bala, B. (2006). Marketing system for apple in hills problems and prospects (A case study of Kullu district, Himachal Pradesh, *Indian Journal of Agricultural Marketing.* **8**(5): 285-293.

Ballington, J.R.; Poling, B. and Olive, K. (2008). Day-neutral strawberry production for season Extension in the Midsouth. *Hortscience.* **43**(7): 1982–1986.

Banaeian, N.; Omid, M. and Ahmadi, H. (2011). Energy and economic analysis o greenhouse strawberry production in Tehran province of Iran, *Energy Conver Manage.*, **52**(2): 1020-1025.

Banaeian, N.; Omid, M. and Ahmadi, H. (2011). Improvement of cost efficiency ir strawberry greenhouses by data envelopment analysis. *Agricultura Tropica E Subtropica.*, **44**(3): 144-146.

Barat, M.M. (2011). Marketing margins of strawberries 2006-2010 shipping poin – terminal – retail price. M. Sc. Thesis, Submitted to Slovak University o Agriculture, Arkansas, Slovak.

Bhat, A.; Kachroo, J. and Kachroo, D. (2011). Economic appraisal of kinnow production and its marketing under North-Western Himalayan region o Jammu. *Agricultural economics research review,* **24**: 283-290. July-December.

Bhat, A.; Kachroo, J. and Kachroo, D. (2011). Economic evaluation of production and marketing of lemon in Kathua district of Jammu and Kashmir state. *Economic Affair,***56**(4): 431-436. December.

Bhat, J. (2010). Problem of apple marketing in Kashmir. *Journal of Research in Commerce and Management.* **01**(6): 105-111. *ISSN* 2277-1166.

Bruchhaus, M.N. (2005). An assessment of consumer preferences for Louisiana strawberries. M.Sc. Thesis Submitted to Graduate Faculty of the Louisiana State University and Agricultural and Mechanical College, LA.

Chand, K.; Dastagiri, M.B.; Gajja, B.L. and Jangid, B.L. (2010). Price spread, marketing efficiency and constraints of carrot marketing in Rajasthan. *Indian Journal of Agricultural Marketing,* **24** (3): 131-142.

Charnes A, WW Cooper and EL Rhodes (1978). "Measuring the Efficiency of Decision Making Units." *EJOR* 2: 429-444.

Chavan, A.B. (1997). Marketing of strawberry in Satara district of Maharashtra, Unpublished M.Sc.(Agri.) thesis, Department of Agricultural Economics, Mahatma Phule Krishi Vidyapeeth, Rahuri (India).

Cooper WW, LM Seiford and J Zhu (2004). Handbook on Data Envelopment Analysis, Kluwer Academic.

Dhandhalya, M.G. and Shiyani, R.L. (2012). Economic viability of sapota orchard and marketing constraints of sapota (Achras Sapota L.) in Saurashtra region. *Indian Journal of Agricultural Marketing,* **26** (1): 179-190.

Dhar Lakshmi. (2010). Economics of pineapple marketing in Meghalaya. CAU *Research Newsletter*. January - June.

Engelseth, P.; Karlsen, A. and Verwaart, T. (2011). Modelling fresh strawberry supply "from-farm-to-fork" as a complex adaptive network. 5th International European Forum on System Dynamics and Innovation in Food Networks. pp. 14-18, February, 2011.

Food and Agriculture Organisation (FAOSTAT).

Galic, D.; Milic, D. and Sredojevic, Z. (2014). Financial results achieved in short day strawberry production. *Economics of Agriculture.* **61**(4): 851-859.

Galleta and Bringhurst. (1995). Small fruit culture and nutritional value. The AV publishing west report. 5th edition, USA: 357.

Gandhi, V.P. and Namboodiri, N.V. (2002). Fruit and vegetable marketing and its efficiency in India: A study of wholesale market in the Ahmadabad Area. *Indian institute of Management, Ahmadabad*: 1-29.

Goyal, P.; Goyal, M. and Singh, A. (2012). Marketing practices of kinnow farmers in Punjab. *International Research Journal of Agricultural Economics and Statistics.* **3**(2): 249-252.

Hatai, L.D. and Naik, D. (2013). Marketing strategy and supply chain analysis of pineapple: A case study in West Garo Hill of Meghalaya. *National seminar on Agri-business potentials in North Eastern States,* pp. 24-25. November: 8-9.

Jafar, A.A.; and Patil, V.A. (2013). A study of cost structure and pricing of strawberry farming in selected villages of Mahabaleshwer Taluka (Dist – Satara). *Tactful Management Research Journal,* **1**(9):1-8.

Jairath, M.S. (2004). Agricultural marketing infrastructural facilities in India. *Indian Journal of Agricultural Marketing.* Conference special **18** (3): 52-63.

Kambara, M.K. and Shelley, L.C. (2002). The California Agricultural Direct Marketing Study. U.S. Department of Agriculture. Agricultural Marketing Service. Transportation and Marketing Programs. Marketing Services Branch. California Institute of Rural Studies Davis, California.

Kaur, H. and Singh, I.P. (2010). Marketing of Kinnow in Sri Ganganagar district of Rajasthan state. *Indian Journal of Agricultural Marketing,* **24** (1): 141-149.

Kaur, M. and Singla, N. (2016). An economic analysis of kinnow cultivation and marketing in Fazilka district of Punjab. *Indian Journal of Economics and Development,* **12** (4): 711-718.

Kaur, S. and Gupta, S. (2013). Price spread in the marketing of fruits in Chandigarh. Research link – 107, *An International Journal,* **XI** (12): 103-105. February.

Keerthi, H.R. (2008). Production and marketing of Pineapple in Shimoga District- An Economic Analysis. *M. Sc.Thesis submitted to the University of Agricultural Sciences, Dharwad.*

Kerutagi, M.G.; Ramchandra, V.A.; Kunnal, L.B.; Mahajanshetti, S.B. and Shirol, A.M. (2009). Marketing of sapota in Northern Karnataka. *Indian Journal of Agricultural Marketing.* **23**(2): 57-63.

Kharche, R.M. (1994). Strawberry: Production technology and marketing, 1st edition, Dwarka Prakashan, Pune.

Kharse, Y.T.; Lohar, N.S.; Babar, V.S. and Bhosale, G.M. (1995). Economics of production and marketing of strawberry in Kolhapur region, AGRESCO Report, MPKV, Rahuri, pp.: 245-250.

Kichu, Y. and Sharma, A. (2014). Economics and constraint of pineapple cultivation in Dimapur district of Nagaland. *Agri-Business Potentials in India. Experience from the hill states*: 217-223.

Kumar, K. and Singh, H.L. (2010). Price spread of Mango in Lucknow district o U.P. *Indian Jouranl of Agricultural Marketing,* **24** (2): 50-57.

Kumar, R.; Sharma, N.; Jamwal, M.; Sharma, R.M.; Singh, D.B. and Parmar, A.M (2012). Production and economic studies of PBRs treated strawberry (*Fragaria x ananassa* duch.) cv. Sweet Charlie. **12**(12): 1543-1547.

Kumbhar, J.S.; Pawar, P.P.; Patole, S.D. and Gavali, A.S. (2014). Economics o production and marketing of guava in Maharashtra. *International Journal o Agricultural Science.* **10**(2): 592-599.

Kumthekar, D.M. and Jafar, A.A. (2016). Problems of strawberry production in Satara district. *Prime International Research Journal.* **3**(4): 16-28.

Kurkute, B.V.; Shendage, P.N.; Jadhav and Nirgude, R.R. (2010). Marketing o banana in Pune district of Maharashtra. *Indian Journal of Agricultural Marketing* **24**(2): 178-187.

Ladaniya, M.S.; Wanjari, V. and Mahalle, B.C. (2003). Price spread of Pomegranate *Indian Journal of Agricultural Economics,* **58**(3): 800-811.

Ladaniya, M.S.; Wanjari, V. and Mahalle, B.C. (2005). Marketing of grapes and raisins and post-harvest losses of fresh grapes in Maharashtra. *Indian J. Agric Res.,* **39**(3): 167–176.

Loghmanpor, R.; Tabatabaekoloor, R., and Asadollah, A. (2013). Input-output energy and economic analysis of strawberry production in Iran. *American Journal of Engineering Research,***2**(5): 173-177.

Mali, A.N. and Kharse, V.T. (1994). Economics of production and marketing of strawberry in Pune district –A case study. AGRESCO Report, MPKV, Rahuri pp.: 128-133.

Mavi, H.K.; Sidha, R.S. and Sidhu, J. S. (2012). Investigating the efficiency of various marketing models and problems of Kinnow growers of Punjab. *Agricultural Economics Research Review,* **25**(1): 87-97.

Mittal Surabhi. (2007). *Can Horticulture be a success story for India?* Working paper 197, August 2007.

Muliar, D.; Singh, Ram and Feroze, S.M. (2017). An economic appraisal of Strawberry Orchard in Meghalaya. *Economic Affairs,* **62**(1):113-119.

Murthy, D.S.; Gajanana, T.M.; Sudha and Subramanyam, K.V. (2009). Post-harvest loss estimation in mangoes, pomegranate and grapes at different stages of marketing- A methodological perspective. *Agricultural Economics Research Review,* **15**(2): 188-200.

Naikawadi, D.J. (1995). Economics of production and marketing of strawberry- A case study in Pune district. AGRESCO Report, MPKV, Rahuri, pp.: 239-244.

Naphade, S.A. and Tingre, A.S. (2008). Economics of production and marketing of guava in Buldhana district of Maharashtra. *Indian Journal of Agricultural Marketing,* **22** (2): 33-41.

National Horticulture Board, Statistics Annual Report 2001-02 to 2015-16. National Horticultural Research and Development Foundation, (nhrdf.org.).

Naveen, B.S. (2009). Economics of production and value addition to wine grapes in Bijapur district of Karnataka. M.Sc. Thesis submitted to University of Agriculture Sciences, Dharwad, Karnataka.

Oladapo, M.O.; Momoh, S.; Yusuf, S. and Awoyinka, Y. (2007). Marketing margin and spatial pricing efficiency of pineapple in Nigeria. *Asian J. Market,***1**: 14-22.

Paranjpe, A. and Cantliffe, D.J. (2004). Economic feasibility of producing strawberry in a passively ventilated greenhouse in North-Central Florida. *Pro. Fla. State. Hort. Soc.,* 117: 27-37.

Prakash, Shiv and Sarkar, D. (2017). Production economics of strawberry in Haryana, India. *Economic Affairs,* **62**(4): 697-704.

Prakash, Shiv; Sarkar, D.; Bishnoi, D.K. and Singh Ram (2018). Production marketing challenges of strawberry cultivation in Haryana. *Indian Journal of Economics and Development,* **14**(1a): 223-226.

Prasher, R.S.; Chandel, S. and Thakur, R. (2013). Economic appraisal of production and marketing of litchi in Himachal Pradesh. *Indian Journal of Agricultural Marketing,* **27** (2): 1-13.

Ramanan, G. (2012). Cost of production and capital productivity of grape cultivation in Tamilnadu, India. *Indian Streams research Journal.* **2**(1): 1-4.

Randev, A.K. (2005). Marketing of apple in Shimla district of Himachal Pradesh. *Indian Journal of Agricultural Marketing,* **19**(3): 11-19.

Rane, A.A. and Bagade, S.R. (2006). Economics of production and marketing of banana in Sindhur district Maharashtra. *Indian Journal of Agricultural Marketing,***20** (1): 38-45.

Rangi, P.S. and Sidhu, M.S. (2004). Development of market infrastructure for globalisation in India. *Indian Journal of Agricultural Marketing.* Conference special **18** (3): 1-21.

Rao, Parthasarathy, P. and Singh, Birthal Prakash (2009). Marketing of Agricultural produce in rainfed regions of India: Emerging scenario. *Indian Journal of Agricultural Marketing.* Conference special **23** (3): 125- 39.

Rauf, A.; Saraf, S.A. and Wani, S.A. (2011). Economics of production and marketing of apple in Himachal Pradesh and Jammu and Kashmir- a comprehensive study. *Indian Journal of Agricultural Marketing,* **25** (1): 97-119.

Rymbai, D.; Singh, R.; Feroze, S.M.; Rani, P.M.N. and Bardoloi, R. (2013). Utilization pattern and marketed surplus of pineapple in Ri-Bhoi district of Meghalaya. *Indian Journal of Agricultural Marketing,* **27** (2): 35-39.

Sachdeva, S.; Tilak, R.S. and Sachdeva, R. (2013) Increasing fruit and vegetable consumption: Challenges and opportunity. *Indian Journal of Community Medicine,* **38**(4): 192-197.

Safley, C.D.; Poling, E.B.; Wohlgenant, M.K. and William, R.F. (2004). What make direct-market strawberry farm successful? North Carolina Cooperative Extension Service. North Carolina State University, North Carolina A and T State University, US department of agriculture and local government cooperating.

Salami, P.; Ahmadi, H. and Keyhani, A. (2010). Energy use and economic analysis of strawberry production in Sanandaj zone of Iran. *Biotechnol. Agron. Soc. Environ.,* **14**(4): 653-658.

Sasane, V.G. (1998). Cost of production and marketing of strawberry in Satara district of Maharashtra. Unpublished M.Sc.(Agri) Department of Agricultural Economics, Mahatma Phule Krishi Vidyapeeth, Rahuri (India).

Sedaghat, R. (2011). Constraints in production and marketing of Iran's Pistachio and the policies concerned: An application of the Garrett Ranking Technique. *International journal of nuts and Related Sciences,* **2**(1): 27-30.

Sekhon, N.S. (2005). Marketing of pear in Amritsar district of Punjab.Unpublished M.Sc. thesis, PAU, Ludhiana.

Shah, D. (2000). Marketing pattern of grapes in Maharashtra- An appraisal. *Indian Journal of Agricultural Marketing,* **14**(1): 40-48.

Shankar, B.S.; Devajar, M. and Rangaswami, R.S.C. (2008). Marketing of grapes in Karnataka: A case study of Bangalore and Bijapur district. *Indian Journal of Marketing,* **38**(2): 40-48.

Singh, B.B.; Singh, K.P.; Singh, D.K. and Roy, D.P. (1990). Marketing of pineapple in North Tripura. *Indian Journal of Agricultural Marketing,* **4** (2): 210-217.

Singh, R.; Feroze, S.M.; Raju, V.T. and Dkhar, D.S. (2012). Agribusiness opportunities in north eastern hills of India: A case study of strawberry growers of Meghalaya. Indian society of agricultural marketing, Nagpur and Kumaun University, Nainital.

Singh, R.S. and Shrivastava, P. (2003). Production and marketing of pineapple in Meghalaya. *Indian Journal of Agricultural Marketing,* Conference special: 158-160.

Singh, S. B.; Choudhury, A. and Singh, S. P. (2013). Production and marketing of passion fruit in Manipur: Some policy issues. *National Seminar on Agri-business potentials in North Eastern States,* pp. 24. November: 8-9.

Srivastav, S.C. and Mishra, R.R. (2001). Price spread and marketing channel of mango in Varanasi district of Uttar Pradesh. *The Bihar Journal of Agricultural Marketing.* **9**(3): 273-280.

Subramanyam, K.V. and Gajanana, T.M. (2000). Cooperative marketing of fruits and vegetables in India. Concept Publishing House, New Delhi.

Thamizhselvan, K. and Murugan, S.P. (2012). Marketing of grapes in Theni district. *IJMT.*,**2**(9): 96-111. ISSN 2249-1058.

Vairam, R. and Muniyandi, B. (2013). An economic analysis of the production and marketing of grape cultivation in Theni district, Tamil Nadu. *IJRCM.*,**03**(9): 14-18. ISSN 2231-4245.

Wanjari, V. and Ladaniya, M.S. (2004). Marketing of banana in selected districts of India. *Tropical Agricultural Research and Extension*. **7**: 126-133.

Websites

http://en.wikipedia.org/wiki/Hisar_district accessed on 04.02.2017

http://bhiwani.nic.in/accessed on 04.02.2017

http://www.choosemyplate.gov

http://www.newkerala.com/states-of-india/haryana.php accessed on 05.02.2017

http://docslide.us/documents/henry-garrett-ranking-techniques. html

http://www.scribd.com/doc/47487605/Henry-Garrett-Ranking-Techniques.

http://shodhganga.inflibnet.ac.in/handle/10603/203288

http://www.indianjournals.com/ijor.aspx?target=ijor:ijed1 and volume=14 and issue=1a and article=037

http://ndpublisher.in/admin/issues/EAv62n1o.pdf

https://projects.ncsu.edu/project/arepublication/ag645_final.pdf

https://pdfs.semanticscholar.org/d439/0b1979803181640c0b84e50fa1237fe5b5e6.pdf

http://ndpublisher.in/lastissuearticle.php?journal=EA and issue=Issue per cent 204 and volume=Volume per cent 2062

http://krishikosh.egranth.ac.in/bitstream/1/81154/1/T03757.pdf

https://mafiadoc.com/cost-and-revenue-analysis-of-strawberry-production-in-the-sub-_59b979fa1723dddac6d89087.html

http://en.wikipedia.org/wiki/Hisar_district

Index